# TAKE YOUR POWER BACK
Healing Lessons, Tips, and Tools for Abuse Survivors

Evelyn M. Ryan

**TAKE YOUR POWER BACK**
**HEALING LESSONS, TIPS, AND TOOLS FOR ABUSE SURVIVORS**

Copyright © 2015 Evelyn M. Ryan.

All rights reserved. No part of this book may be used or reproduced by any means, graphic, electronic, or mechanical, including photocopying, recording, taping or by any information storage retrieval system without the written permission of the author except in the case of brief quotations embodied in critical articles and reviews.

Please join the Yourlifelifter Community at:
https://yourlifelifter.wordpress.com and
https://www.facebook.com/yourlifelifter

Disclaimer:
Information contained in this book does not constitute or replace any medical, legal, financial, or any other form of professional advice.
The information contained herein does not replace any medical or psychiatric treatment. If you believe you may have a condition, please seek qualified professional advice and care.

iUniverse books may be ordered through booksellers or by contacting:

iUniverse
1663 Liberty Drive
Bloomington, IN 47403
www.iuniverse.com
1-800-Authors (1-800-288-4677)

Because of the dynamic nature of the Internet, any web addresses or links contained in this book may have changed since publication and may no longer be valid. The views expressed in this work are solely those of the author and do not necessarily reflect the views of the publisher, and the publisher hereby disclaims any responsibility for them.

Any people depicted in stock imagery provided by Thinkstock are models, and such images are being used for illustrative purposes only.
Certain stock imagery © Thinkstock.

ISBN: 978-1-4917-7816-6 (sc)
ISBN: 978-1-4917-7817-3 (hc)
ISBN: 978-1-4917-7815-9 (e)

Library of Congress Control Number: 2015915988

Print information available on the last page.

iUniverse rev. date: 11/16/2015

I dedicate this book to my mother, my aunt Sophie, and my beloved friend Lezlie, who inspired me to follow my dreams and taught me the true meaning of compassion and unconditional love. I also dedicate this book to other courageous survivors who took their power back, broke the cycle of intergenerational abuse, and serve as beacons of light to those who are searching in the dark.

# Contents

Preface ............................................................................... ix
Introduction ....................................................................... xi

| | | |
|---|---|---|
| Chapter 1 | The Real Truth about Abuse and Healing ............ 1 |
| Chapter 2 | Healing Lessons ................................................. 17 |
| Chapter 3 | The Healing and Recovery Journey ................... 40 |
| Chapter 4 | Recovering from Traumatic Stress and Toxic Shame and Grief ................................................. 50 |
| Chapter 5 | Building Self-Esteem and Self-Compassion ........ 65 |
| Chapter 6 | You Have Taken Your Power Back and You Are Thriving ................................................ 76 |
| Appendix 1 | Self-Help Healing Tools .................................... 81 |
| Appendix 2 | Inspirational Healing Messages ....................... 123 |

Bibliography ............................................................................ 131

# Preface

I wrote this book to feed my lifelong passion for truth and to help adult survivors of childhood and adult abuse and other traumas heal from what I refer to as "pain addictions."

*Take Your Power Back* is based on skills and knowledge gained through personal healing; over twenty years of study on abuse, trauma, and personality disorders; and thirty-five years as an authority on solving problems in high-risk industries to get to the specific root causes of abuse and the harm it does to victims throughout their childhood and into adulthood.

This book exposes the lies we all have been living. It will help you discover that the source of truth-based healing resides within you—within each and every one of us—and learn how to tap into that infinite power.

I share with you the most current, proven, and effective lessons, tips, and tools that have helped me in my journey and been validated collectively by the tens of thousands of skilled psychology professionals and abuse victims around the world I interact with daily.

My personal goal is to help you use the knowledge contained in this book to find your personal truth, regain your personal power, release your emotional pain, end your suffering, and become the best version of yourself you were put on this earth to be—always with my blessings!

# Introduction

*You cannot heal at the same level of thinking that created your pain.*

If you are reading this, you are most likely unhappy, emotionally fatigued, and suffering from chronic emotional pain. Perhaps you are in the middle of an emotional crisis brought on by death, betrayal, illness, or divorce—or perhaps you are just ready to heal because you have had enough. You are seeking answers, the real truth, because your actions and decisions are not and have not been serving you well. You have come to the right place!

Victims of adult abuse were victims of childhood abuse, covert or overt. You were conditioned that being in pain is normal. This may have helped you cope, adapt, and survive in the short term—in that moment of childhood defenselessness—but in the long term, it has made you continue to think like a victim, like someone who deserves pain and has no power to overcome it. As a child, you learned to abandon yourself, to be consumed with shame and self-blame. When you became an adult, you allowed reliance on others, drugs, alcohol, gambling, or material things—rather than yourself—to define your self-worth and soothe your pain.

Instead of living, you learned to just exist. On an unconscious level, you created a false version of yourself to make you acceptable to others. Your decisions and perceptions became fear-, shame-, and anxiety-based rather than truth-based, and they did not result in sustainable emotional gains and improvements in your life. You learned to mal-adapt and believe—falsely—that you did not deserve better. As a result, you never pursued better. Your belief system became skewed, and your self-compassion, self-esteem, self-worth, self-love, and self-respect suffered.

You did not thrive because you were not your authentic self. You were reactive; your actions originated in others' expectations and needs and your internalized ideal of how you should be, not from how you really were. You saw other people or things as the cause and/or the solution to your problems.

You learned to settle in your choice of job, career, finances, goals, and partner. You learned to self-medicate to alleviate the internal pain, shame, and self-loathing. Prolonged self-alienation, neglect of personal needs, and exposure to shame led to depression. In essence, your beliefs became a self-fulfilling prophecy.

If you find yourself constantly returning to a state of pain that you believe (falsely) you are deserving of and powerless to prevent, now is the time to face the real truth and turn this vicious cycle into a victor's circle. You do not need all the answers to move forward. I am here to tell you that *you are no longer a victim*. You will heal and recover, and you are more than deserving and worthy of doing so.

Healing and recovery, my friends, are part of the process of self-discovery, a process of re-owning ourselves by uncovering the root causes of our suffering so we can heal the wounds and release the pain once and for all. The only person we are here to serve is our authentic self. When we do, all life's pieces fall into place, because our decisions and actions are truth-based and serve ourselves.

Your self-compassion, self-esteem, self-worth, self-love, self-respect, and self-esteem will soar. These behaviors are not selfish, as many of us were raised to believe. Rather, they are what the psychological community calls adaptive and emotionally healthy. Healing through self-discovery helps us become emotionally fit by introducing us to our authentic, self-assured selves. Self-discovery is a learning process.

*Take Your Power Back* gets down to the origin of abuse and clarifies the harm it does to its victims throughout childhood and into adulthood. It will teach you to re-own the self that you long ago abandoned. By accepting your powerlessness, challenging your thoughts, releasing your fears and shame, and incrementally taking your power back, you will finally discover and honor your real self and your personal divinity. In the healing process, you will regain your trust, self-respect, and self-esteem.

Asking the right questions and finding truthful answers in a safe and trusting environment lead us to turn our compassion and courage inward. Shifts in our thinking contribute to short- and long-term emotional health and happiness. We discover, in the process, our true value. We learn to rely on and trust internal cues that have been recalibrated with our newfound personal truth and core beliefs. We rescue ourselves incrementally from the depths of despair, begin to rely on our own abilities, and feel safe in our bodies again.

Of course, we must get feedback from our environment—from others who have our best interests at heart. In this way, we will be better equipped to recognize those who do not. We now can readily gauge emotions and recalibrate internal truth-seeking filters based on choices that we trust to serve us well and maintain and sustain our well-being.

So in healing, we learn who we really are, and to love ourselves. We learn to accept ourselves, warts and all, as enough—perfect in our being—without self-criticism and fault-finding judgment. We learn to do the following:

- cultivate vitality, courage, and self-respect
- think like a winner, not a victim
- formulate opinions and values that are our own
- take informed risks and make decisions based on our own internal cues, which we trust and rely on
- take ourselves back, to re-own ourselves
- do what we want and need to do rather than what others expect of us
- trust and regulate our emotions
- care for ourselves and respect our own and others' personal rights and authority

- use our compassion for ourselves and others responsibly
- become resilient and bounce back quickly from setbacks

I am so happy you are here and seeking answers—truthful ones, not the glittery versions. I want you to be successful. I want you to thrive. I am a huge advocate for your successful healing journey and a faithful believer in your worthiness for a joy-seeking rather than a pain-seeking/avoiding life.

Before you start on your healing journey, read chapter 1 to learn the real truth about abuse and the harm it does to the thinking and beliefs we bring with us into adulthood.

Next, read the fundamental lessons or truths in chapter 2 that challenge what I believe are the biggest falsehoods in thinking that can hinder your healing.

Move on to chapter 3, which maps out your step-by-step healing journey—including where to start—and offers basic lessons, tips, and tools to heal your emotional wounds, build your self-esteem, break your pain addictions, and teach effective coping skills.

Chapters 4 through 7 and the appendices offer a more detailed and comprehensive set of lessons, tools, tips, and inspirations to choose from to support your healing journey, help you achieve your goals, and monitor your progress.

Move forward in your life. Thrive and be the joy-filled person you were put on this earth to be. Healing allows you to become the best version of yourself. It is the best demonstration of self-love you can give yourself. In that newfound truth, we thrive.

May your spiritual source guide and protect you in your search for truth. I wish you all blessings in your journey and in your life.

Together we heal! Together we thrive!

*Evely*

# Chapter 1

# The Real Truth about Abuse and Healing

Adult survivors of childhood abuse become adult victims of adulthood abuse because they continue to think like victims. This is not a role anyone consciously chooses; rather, it is one we learned in childhood when our brains were developing. We were defenseless against the pain inflicted upon us, and so we took subconscious wounds and pain-based beliefs of unworthiness with us into adulthood.

We became addicted to pain and dependent on unreliable people's approval to define our worthiness. Rather than being in control of our own adult lives, we showed up with deep-seated hidden vulnerabilities we were not aware of that caused us to become complicit in our continued abuse. Our brains were traumatized while they were still developing; our trauma, shame, and grief emotions were overstressed. We developed a false belief in our powerlessness over our exaggerated, pain-based emotions, and an equally a false belief that we were unlovable and must suffer and sacrifice ourselves to be loved.

We became chronically fearful because we overestimated danger (that we expected to come) and underestimated our ability to deal with it. We became hypervigilant and did not feel safe in our own bodies. We thought we deserved pain, and we did not authentically pursue joy because we believed we were not worthy of better. We abandoned our own selves and learned to rely on others for our survival and self-worth.

We perpetuated abuse through the generations as we taught these faulty thinking patterns that had been passed on to us to our children. We and our children ended up neurotic, addicted, or codependent. We became targets of emotional predators, including bullies, manipulators, con artists, narcissists, and psychopaths who preyed on our vulnerabilities in our jobs, schools, churches, neighborhoods, relationships, and everyday lives.

We invested most of our time and energy in avoiding pain and living lies. However, this did not nurture our emotional needs or heal our deep-seated wounds. We continued to suffer. We learned to feel unsafe in our own bodies and abandon our own selves. We became emotionally exhausted. We fell into depression. We learned the hard way that pretending or acting like we were happy was not the same as happiness.

Abuse is an interdependent relationship between abusers and victims. As long as victims allow it, abusers continue to abuse. As long as victims allow themselves to be victimized, they continue to be victims. Abusers trigger the inner childhood feelings of unworthiness repressed in our unconscious minds, and we react as we did in childhood. We believe falsely that we are powerless to the pain and turn our power over to the abusers, trying to appease them to regain their approval. Our abusers become the cause of and the solution to our pain.

An emotionally healthy person would not tolerate the abuse; he or she would not rely on an abuser to validate worthiness or alleviate pain. An emotionally healthy partner would remind us of and help us nurture our self-assurance and self-reliance.

Interestingly enough, abusers and abuse victims are similar. Both use others to cope, self-soothe, and avoid pain. Both typically have very low self-esteem and self-respect; they are not able to tap into their personal strength. Both believe falsely that they are powerless. Both believe they cannot generate their own power and sense of self-worth. Each triggers the other's fears, and the toxic abuse cycle continues.

However, there is one fundamental difference between abusers and abuse victims: abusers offensively and intentionally *take* power from their victims to relieve their pain, while victims defensively and unintentionally *give up* their power to abusers to relieve their emotional pain. In an attempt to release deep-seated emotional discomfort, both abusers and abuse victims develop toxic coping mechanisms that keep them in pain and perpetuate the harm done to themselves and others.

**Abusers Target Their Victims**

An abusive relationship is a predatory one. Victims' vulnerabilities make them targets of abusers, bullies, and covert aggressive manipulators like narcissists and psychopaths who aggressively seek, pursue, and feed off of them. Victims, sadly, become unknowingly complicit in their abuse and suffering, and they prolong the chronic emotional pain they feel powerless to stop. Being in emotional pain and distress becomes a normal way of life. Relationships and other people become sources or solutions to pain—or both. The solution becomes the perpetuating cause of the problem.

Victims become codependents, reliant on others to define their self-worth and relieve the unrelenting pain. Their false sense of powerlessness, originating in childhood, holds them captive. Traumatic stress, grief, and shame become their emotional drugs of choice. Victims may even prefer the pain of an abusive relationship to the pain and fear they experience in solitude. They may believe that pain is easier to manage.

Victims and abusers can become addicted to alcohol, drugs, people, or material things and develop neurotic compulsions or phobias for the purpose of self-soothing. Victims develop stress disorders and physical ailments. They become prisoners of their pain and false fears. Adult victims teach distorted pain- and fear-driven thinking patterns to their children and perpetuate generational abuse.

Our miraculous brains are capable of so much, but they are not very effective at spontaneous emotional healing. If we try to mask or deny deep-seated pain, it will raise its ugly head when we least expect it, most likely during a personal tragedy or crisis. The good news is that victims of childhood abuse and other traumas have the power to heal and recover from their emotional wounds and distorted thinking. We can stop thinking like victims and achieve emotional freedom—what addiction therapist Glynis Sherwood refers to as "emotional sobriety."

When we release the pain and take our power back, the abuse stops. The pain stops. Our children learn to heal through us, so intergenerational abuse stops.

**The Journey to Emotional Healing**

No matter where we are in our personal journey, we struggle for the same reasons: We suffered immeasurable trauma when we were ill-equipped to deal with it. We were betrayed by people we intimately loved and trusted in our childhood, and those patterns continued into our adulthood.

Abuse in any form—including neglect, abandonment, and invalidation of our emotions—is betrayal. We learned in childhood to abandon our own selves. Our self-esteem and self-worth plummeted. We became emotionally wounded by and bonded to our abusers. We suffered chronic emotional pain. We become addicted to pain.

Our wounds are the same. Our stories are the same—different town, different city, different country, same pain. Adult survivors of childhood abuse suffer into adulthood because our protective pain and fear emotions went haywire when our brains were still developing. Pain became a chronic addiction. We continue to suffer through adolescence and into adulthood with exaggerated pain and fear. We believe falsely that we are the source of this pain—and that we not only deserve it but are also defenseless against it.

However, abuse and suffering are not a life sentence. We *can* survive and thrive after abuse. Our brains can heal, and we can heal—and through us, so can our children. We can learn to stop thinking like victims and protect ourselves from those who prey and attack and betray us, including our own selves. In healing, we return to our original condition, our authentic selves. Just as it took time for the negative impact to affect us, so it will take time to restore our health, achieve emotional sobriety, and gain emotional freedom from our pain addiction.

Healing is the kind of noble effort we are not accustomed to making. We are used to routinely sacrificing and giving too much of our time, energy, money, compassion, love, and effort to others—many of whom are unworthy, and abuse and manipulate us. So how are we to heal and stop being victims if we only know how to think like and be victims? How do we, after a lifetime of abuse, find a way to heal if we do not know what emotional sobriety looks like and feels like? How do we embrace it if we do not believe we are worthy? How are we to heal if we do not know why these things happened to us and continue to blame ourselves and feel ashamed? How do we heal if we are dependent on others to define our power and self-worth? How do we get off the emotional roller-coaster of pain and break this cycle?

We cannot heal our psychological wounds and end compulsive self-destructive behaviors at the same level of thinking that caused our pain. Healing requires major shifts in our thinking to address our authentic needs. It calls for commitment, compassion, tolerance, hard work, and dedication. This will vary from person to person; the degree of pain is different for each of us, and we all learn and process information differently. Get ready to work the hardest you ever have and to challenge who you are and what you feel, think, and believe. Now is the time to focus your compassion on yourself.

Healing requires self-focus. We must challenge thought processes and beliefs that we are not accustomed to questioning—that in previous relationships, we were punished for questioning. Healing involves a leap of faith. It invites us to detach from what we are comfortable being, believing, thinking, and doing. It calls us to face and challenge the familiar sources of pain and fear, and to embrace new beliefs with which we are not so familiar.

In restoring our emotional health after abuse, we are challenged to break addictions to our own pain and replace our faulty thinking patterns with healthy ones so we can take care of our emotional needs. Sherwood puts it this way in "Emotional Sobriety: The Golden Key to Addiction Recovery":

> People who engage in addictive behaviors are often out of touch with—and therefore at a loss about—how to care for their emotional needs ... When emotions are associated with crisis or pain, people can become "emotion-phobic," and want to escape or avoid feelings through "self-medicating" addictive behavior. They may turn to alcohol, drugs, food, relationships, or the Internet to try and achieve a sense of gratification and calm. The solution becomes the problem, however, as legitimate psychological needs continue to go unmet, and difficulties escalate into the crisis of addiction.

So I will caution you that healing will most likely feel very uncomfortable and even painful at first. In time, it will get easier and easier as you achieve each healing milestone and regain your personal strength, confidence in your abilities, and coping ability. Be gentle with yourself. Be trusting and accepting of yourself without judgment. Turn your compassion and empathy and patience inward and treat yourself as you would a small child who is learning to crawl or walk for the first time.

Healing calls us to acknowledge our powerlessness over pain and to access (and release) the sources of pain that can bring us to a state of utter despair. This allows us to rely on ourselves—for some, this may be the first time—and commit to using our strength for our own personal benefit. This is how we change negative thought patterns to positive ones and reprogram our victim-thinking to the mind-set of winners and thrivers. This is how all folks with addictions (and pain for abuse victims is an addiction) recover.

As you discover and come into your own truth, you will gain the following:

- emotional strength as your self-confidence and self-assurance build
- an awareness of what triggers your painful emotions and moods, and an improved ability to cope with them before the pain escalates
- more responsiveness to outside influences as you become less reactive
- a feeling of safety in your own body
- confidence in your ability to consciously choose your response to situations that are in your best interest with due consideration for others, rather than emotionally gambling by unconsciously reacting in unhealthy ways to gain others' approval and avoid pain

Mentors, coaches, and therapists can be instrumental in guiding you through the process, but the answers to truth-based healing reside in us. We must seek them out and apply them by reaching into the core of our being for the answers. The point is this:

*You must uncover and discover to recover.*

This is how we break addictions to our pain and achieve emotional sobriety. This is how we heal. This is how we take our power back. This is how we become who we really are.

## The Role of Self-Discovery and Self-Recovery in Emotional Healing

In self-discovery, we deploy a healing plan for psychological wellness and transition from victim to survivor. We develop the skills, confidence, resilience, and self-respect that come from dealing with our emotions directly and effectively, rather than compulsively with behaviors that cause us pain and fear. Self-discovery calls us to abandon the false version of ourselves—not in order to serve others, but to serve ourselves. We wipe our thinking slates clean, address our emotional challenges, reverse our faulty thinking, and start a "new you" from scratch.

The goal of self-discovery is to heal emotional wounds from our past and present, and to develop effective strategies to stop the pain that holds us captive to our emotions. We must tailor the steps and milestones in our healing to our unique individual needs. Sherwood explains in her report "Stop the Struggle: Five Steps to Breaking Free from Chronic Emotional Pain" that

> the purpose of your emotions is to help you make sense of your life, and to let you know whether something you are experiencing is good, neutral or bad ... If you are aware of your emotions, you can then make informed decisions about whether to continue with your current train of thought or the situation you find yourself in, or to change them for the better ... Learning to identify early warning signs that tell you emotional pain is surfacing will enable you to intervene before problems with stress, anxiety, depression or trauma become overwhelming. You can then face life's challenges—regardless of how long they have been going on—feeling more confident and

hopeful about your ability to cope effectively and feel at peace ...

Through self-evaluation—guided by a competent therapist or self-help strategies—we learn to consciously recognize the sources of our pain and what triggers them, identify our maladaptive coping behaviors, and develop a whole new set of coping skills that foster self-esteem and healthy relationships. This requires us to change our identity from critic to compassionate witness; objectively evaluate our thinking and provide feedback to ourselves; process the results; address and remove the pain-based and fear-based thinking that does not serve us; and shift to truth-based thinking that does.

We must dive deep into our painful pasts and relive painful moments—the sources of our pain, fear, and distorted thinking—that can keep us trapped in destructive self-fulfilling prophecies. We must rescue our long-abandoned selves from our own despair and forgive ourselves without judgment. Self-discovery leads us to tap into courage and strength that we most likely never accessed previously and are uncomfortable with, while challenging the pain, shame, and fear we are all too familiar and comfortable with.

Emotional healing identifies the skills and abilities we lack and pushes our maladaptive fear buttons. Self-observation can be especially difficult for victims of childhood abuse who have an aversion to self-care because in the past, they were neglected and punished for it. We also may be heavily dependent on others rather than ourselves to define our self-worth and have not learned to trust our own judgment. Even common, everyday needs can trigger feelings of intense guilt and shame.

Dr. Marcia Sirota, an expert on treating trauma and addiction, explains in "Post Traumatic Stress in Adult Survivors of Child Abuse" that "on top of the abuse and neglect, denial heaps more hurt upon the child by requiring her to alienate herself from reality and her own experience. In troubled families, abuse and neglect are permitted; it's the talking about them that is forbidden."

We may misinterpret this raw accountability to our healing goals as shame, feel attacked and vulnerable, and unconsciously revert to the familiar pain-avoiding and blaming patterns of victimhood, where we feel safe, where we feel comfortable. Michael A. Wright, PhD, clarifies in "Accountability Is Not Shame, but Guilt Can Be Motivating" that "the problem with shame is that it obscures the desired goals in favor of self-protection or saving-face goals." When our pain-based emotions emerge, it's like turning the house lights on at the end of a show. We all are exposed wherever we are standing and however we look. For abuse victims, this can be terrifying.

The steps to self-discovery are designed to help us regain our personal strength, release the shame, and develop the self-compassion that we need to heal. Self-recovery is a separate but adjunct process in which we learn to rely on our newly discovered truth and inner power to care for and feel safe in our own bodies. In self-recovery, we do the following:

- transition from a survivor to a thriver who is not only able to recognize pain triggers and address them but no longer fears them or feels defenseless toward them
- develop strategies and skills to stop the pain that held us captive
- learn and apply our new skills to release the deep-seated traumatic pain that gets locked in our bodies and subconscious and keeps us trapped in destructive thought patterns and relationships.

So while healing starts with self-discovery, the goals set for self-recovery are achieved not only sequentially but in parallel. One supports the other—what you learn in self-discovery supports self-recovery, and vice versa. Like self-discovery, self-recovery requires courage and strength that reside within us but have atrophied from nonuse.

Embedded sources of pain addiction put our healing at risk and also put us in long-term danger of being unhappy, readily giving up our power, developing other addictions, and being abused again. Traumatic stress and chronic toxic shame and grief are discussed at length in chapter 4. Traumatic pain causes us to surrender our self-esteem, power, and emotions to whatever or whomever triggers them. These traumatic pain sources can cause our healing to fail and keep us bonded to our abusers. Exaggerated pain keeps us codependent and addicted to those who are destructive to us, and to abusive and emotionally unhealthy situations, beliefs, and relationships. We can long for our abusers and even protect them because we embrace trauma and pain—we feel we have more control over these, and we fear abandonment more.

Staying subconsciously trapped in irrational pain and fear (our neuroses) makes us vulnerable to narcissists and other covert aggressors who hunt for and feed off of our vulnerabilities. Read more in Healing Lesson 5 in chapter 2. Exploitive relationships can themselves create addictive trauma bonds. See Healing Lesson 6 in chapter 2.

Chronic traumatic stress and pain are best dealt with in psychotherapy with a skilled counselor; however, through self-help, you can learn personal coping strategies to help you feel less overwhelmed. As we come into the truth of who we are and start to identify and tap into our strengths, we are better able to release our pain and heal deep-seated wounds. As we challenge and overcome the obstacles to our happiness and replace them with healthy, self-serving, loving beliefs, we move toward becoming our authentic selves and start to trust and feel safe in our own bodies again. In regaining that truth, we gain self-respect, self-power, and healing.

As we learn to tap into our own being for its healing power, we begin to self-soothe and heal. As we learn to trust and rely on ourselves and our decisions, emotions, and abilities, we heal. As we learn to surround ourselves with truly loving people who treat us with the respect we deserve, we heal. As we learn to love ourselves and others in reciprocal, emotionally balanced relationships, we heal.

We learn that the strength to heal and the solutions to address whatever emotional challenges we face reside within us, and we learn to take our power back. And in that process we move from victim to survivor to thriver.

## Why Self-Forgiveness Is Fundamental to Healing and Achieving Justice

Abuse victims deal with shame and confusion related to forgiveness and justice. We hear repeatedly that if we do not forgive our attackers, we punish ourselves twice. Our need to forgive can also be driven by our moral, ethical, or religious beliefs and convictions. This can leave us conflicted and compound our existing deep-seated shame when, in reality, we do not want to forgive our attackers.

Forgiving our abusers is a very personal decision. We do not *have* to forgive. However, whatever the case, our level of forgiveness should not excuse the actions of the abusers or the depravity of their actions. Healing and justice are not achieved through excusing the evil or pain of betrayal that was inflicted on us by our attackers or by showing compassion for our abusers. This is denial of the truth and causes us to take on additional pain, blame, and shame. It can hamper our healing and recovery.

We were victims—no different than victims of a crime, a brutal illegal attack, or any other violation of our boundaries, rights, authority, and freedom. What are the differences between a brutal attack on one's body or possessions and one's psyche and one's heart in a betrayal of intimate trust? Not many. But there are a few fundamental ones.

One attack, you may think, takes place in the conscious physical world, the other in the metaphysical—the metacognitive world where we feel and think. The pain, shame, anger, fear, and trauma we experience from a brutal physical or emotional attack are the same. Both inflict the same wounds and frequently open old ones. However, there is a huge difference in how we heal from the wounds.

We can achieve justice and emotional relief when our attackers are found, charged, found guilty, and punished for their deeds. Our victimization is then validated, and with support from the legal community—which has ensured our safety and security—we are free to heal. But what happens when a criminal "gets away with murder" and is free to roam and victimize whomever he or she chooses to target? Isn't this what serial thieves do? Isn't this what serial murderers do? Isn't this what serial abusers do? How do innocent victims get justice when their attackers essentially get off free of charge? How then do they achieve emotional relief and a sense of safety, security, and closure? Victims of emotional abuse do not even have the option of becoming vigilantes because the narcissists, like the mutants in *X-Men* and space creatures in *Men in Black*, look normal on the outside. They do their dirty deeds and roam the earth unscathed.

These fundamental differences impact greatly on how we heal. In essence, not only are we the victims, but we also have to serve as police, judge, and jury. No one said life would be fair. It is what it is. This occurs when we, with compassion, go deep inside our own selves to work on releasing the pain, trauma, shame, anger, and fear that were projected onto us and inflicted on us by the emotional criminals, vampires, and thieves who also stole our identities.

We are left to heal invisible wounds that were caused by our active but unaware participation in our abuse by those who preyed on our emotional vulnerabilities. To heal, we must not only release the pain and anger from the attack but also the shame of betrayal, our unconscious complicity in the crime, and our perceived foolery. This is why self-forgiveness and self-compassion are so important in our recovery. Releasing the shame of our complicity will allow us to heal emotionally because it will free us from the toxic embedded pain that keeps us emotionally trapped.

Forgiveness is part of healing. It is not a prerequisite to healing. It is a point we reach when we understand and accept the truth about what happened to us from a position of emotional neutrality without the pain, blame, and shame that our abusers showered on us. It is not excusing our attackers. It is accepting what happened and letting go of the resentment and thoughts of revenge that cause us to continue to transfer our power and energy to our abusers.

Before we can heal, our focus must be on our own selves. To fully heal, we must accept the role we played in our abuse and forgive ourselves without judgment. Understanding why we were targeted and what makes us vulnerable to attack is critical to healing. It is close to impossible to fully accept what happened to us without judgment until we have healed from the abuse, recovered from the trauma, and stopped believing we are victims.

As a survivor, I can say that I do not excuse the despicable acts of the abusers in my life, but I am clear on what happened and why it happened in my childhood, why I was targeted, and why it continued into my adulthood. I have accepted responsibility for the role I played in my abuse without judgment. I am clear that the abuse no longer continues because I do not think like a victim so I am no longer a victim. I choose not to participate in the dysfunction, so it is diffused and goes away. Abusers continue to target me, but I am not emotionally vested. I no longer fear them. I no longer feel defenseless or powerless, so I am no longer vulnerable.

I no longer believe I have to suffer or sacrifice myself to be good or lovable. I do, however, accept them for the abusers and broken people they are. We cannot expect things from people they are not capable of giving. I accept that life is not fair, and I was born into a family that I had no choice over. But I do have choices now based on my own personal truth and not the lies my attackers conditioned me to believe. I choose a life I know I deserve, a life of peace, harmony, happiness, emotionally healthy love, and mutual respect. I also accept that they cannot. I am emotionally free to see things truthfully, accept what happened to me, take back my personal power, and stop being a victim to emotional criminals. In the process, I achieved the justice I sought: my and my daughter's emotional freedom.

The best revenge is success and ending the cycle of abuse. *This* is how we heal. *This* is how we achieve justice. *This* is how we thrive.

## Our Healing and Recovery Are Gifts to Ourselves

Healing and recovery are personal rebuilding processes that require extreme personal self-sacrifice, similar to childbirth. We must not only parent ourselves but also re-own the selves we have learned to abandon. Healing is the ultimate display of self-love and self-sacrifice, similar to a mother's love for her child.

As we have discussed, this process is painful and requires the courage to turn our compassion inward and put in effort and sacrifice for our own well-being. Courage for victims of abuse involves learning to replace pain and fear with faith in ourselves, an understanding that we are worth our own self-sacrifice, and trust that we deserve the outcome of our efforts. It requires us to learn the roots of our false beliefs, deep-seated pain, and fears that do not serve us. We must release them and replace them with beliefs and emotions that do serve us—replace them with *truth*. This process requires learning what happened to us and why, tapping into our strength, rebuilding our self-esteem, taking back our power, learning to protect our personal boundaries, and using our compassion responsibly.

Healing and recovery provide us an opportunity (and for some it may be the first time) to exercise compassion, self-love, self-care, and self-sacrifice for our own benefit. Recovery requires releasing the pain from our deep-seated trauma wounds—wounds that may not even reach our level of awareness but can keep us addicted to our abusers. You are worth it. We all are worth it. Emotional freedom is wonderful, and you deserve it.

In effect, our abuse provides a raw opportunity to face our internal demons, defeat them, and become the best versions of ourselves we were put on this earth to be. It provides us an opportunity to honor and respect ourselves and our divinity. It is a painful rebirth, a renewal that we participate in and are witness to. In the process, we take our selves back! How beautiful is that—the ultimate display of self-love and our divinity, a magnificent gift in disguise.

As Kay, a client, told me, "It sounds a bit weird, but I'm actually grateful for the opportunity to be strong and grow as a person. I have asked myself if I could go back to being who I was when I met him, would I do that, and the answer is no. I needed to experience what I did to get to where I am now. Perhaps I should be thanking him for the life lesson."

# Chapter 2

# Healing Lessons

You are ready to embark on your healing journey. You are seeking answers—the real truth, not the glittered version—because your actions, decisions, relationships, jobs, and emotions have not served you well.

As discussed in chapter 1, victims of abuse have been conditioned to think like victims. It is this thinking that hinders recovery. Victims can get so accustomed to living cyclical patterns of seeking and avoiding pain that they do not understand the real extent of their unhappiness and level of dependence on harmful relationships. Our egos have served their protective coping purposes well by shielding us from our real pain, hiding those parts of us we do not want the world to see, and showing to others only what we think they should see. We have grown accustomed to living from a core of shame, lies, falsehoods, pain, and fear that has skewed our reality.

You may live and work in environments where these dysfunctions continue, the boundaries of personal respect are habitually violated, and personal rights are not honored. Your self-esteem suffers, and you live to avoid pain rather than pursue and seek joy. Perhaps you do not even know what brings you joy. The distorted thinking and skewed beliefs that create invisible barriers to your happiness can also create barriers to your healing.

I am a huge advocate for your successful journey and a faithful believer in your worthiness for living a joy-seeking rather than a pain-avoiding life. I want you to be successful! I want you to thrive. Before you embark on your healing journey (chapter 3), here are some fundamental lessons or truths to help you challenge what I believe are the biggest falsehoods in your thinking that have hindered and will continue to create obstacles in your healing journey.

## Healing Lesson 1:
## We Cannot Heal at the Same Level of Thinking That Creates Our Pain

Abuse is the number-one reason people seek psychological counseling. Victims of childhood abuse suffer neuroses from having pain inflicted on them and not being nurtured by those who professed to love them. They bring these neuroses into adulthood. If you are suffering from adult abuse or a major emotional crisis and think you were not abused as a child, think again. Abuse can be covert or overt, aggressive or not aggressive. Neglect is abuse. Emotional abandonment is abuse. Invalidation is abuse. Child victims also repress memories defensively to protect themselves from trauma.

The type and severity of abuse does not make you immune to the harm even if you do not consciously recognize it. Victims of abuse have been conditioned that being in pain is normal. They are taught to think like victims but do not see themselves as victims; they continue to blame themselves for their own pain, which they think they deserve and are powerless to stop.

We are not the source of our pain. We are the source of our joy. Unfortunately, when we are traumatized by childhood abuse, we lose our full capacity to use our emotions to guide healthy decisions and actions. The overwhelmed emotions that helped us cope, adapt, and survive in the short term, in that moment, have made us, in adulthood, continue to think like victims, to think like someone who deserves pain and has no power to deal with it.

We become addicted to pain. The solution becomes the problem because we have not developed the coping skills or beliefs or confidence to rescue ourselves from our own destructive thought patterns. Our emotions and our adult egos, rather than driving us to action, keep us trapped in inaction. Let's explore this.

You are here to heal and recover, and you are more than deserving and worthy of doing so. Healing and recovery involve detaching from and then re-owning yourself. By uncovering the root causes of your pain, you can heal the wounds and release deep-seated pain once and for all. Healing requires fully understanding why we continue to attract and love people who inflict pain on us. We were abused because those we trusted, including our childhood caretakers (who professed to love us), were emotionally unhealthy people who lacked self-esteem and coping skills and projected their pain, shame, and fear onto us. We were abused because our abusers invalidated our emotions.

We, vulnerable, powerless children, abandoned ourselves, became consumed with shame and self-blame, and developed false beliefs about our defectiveness and lack of lovability that we brought into adulthood. We became dependent on abusers who inflicted pain on us to validate our worth. Here is Caryn's repressed memory of a "childhood hurt she will never forget" when her "stepfather went off the deep end."

> I was fourteen. He was frantically pacing the dining room as we—my mother, my father, and I—sat at the table. He was ranting awful things about me ... I remember my father kept telling him to "calm down," my mother sat silently. I sat and wept listening to his filthy, accusatory rage ... I remember the tension. The secrets. The white, purple, pink, black, and blue elephants in the room that were never, ever acknowledged. I had no voice. Nor did my mother ... I grew up in an environment of extreme fear and intimidation: functioning dysfunction, unacknowledged abuse, a complete and total lack of boundaries. This

> was the norm. I knew nothing different … I was depressed and suicidal … Whoever says emotional abuse is a figment of your imagination, or that it wasn't that bad, or that you're too sensitive, go ask that fourteen-year-old girl back in 1986 what that moment felt like. She would tell you she wished for beatings because they were easier, for they were over quickly. She'd tell you she never asked to be born and wished she never was. She fantasized about dying. She'd tell you she wasn't even worth the space she took up in the world … She was a beautiful disaster. Do you ever really fix that, or does it just become part of the quilt of you? Black thread and mis-stitching is part of me. The imperfections are today what make me perfect. Some things will never be right, but I'm okay with that. I'm good. As good as I've ever been.

This gut-wrenchingly describes how, after years of abuse, Caryn became a pain-driven, self-critical version of herself, the version the ones she trusted conditioned her to become in order to serve their selfish needs. In the process, she did not learn how to serve her own needs.

Abuse victims may have one or more sources of pain they need to address. Not everyone suffers from traumatic stress or trauma-bonding or depression, but most all victims suffer from chronic shame and grief, for example. We also typically lack coping and assertiveness skills, self-compassion, and healthy self-esteem.

When we become adults and are worn down from emotional fatigue, we develop neurotic compulsions and become reliant on drugs, alcohol, or someone or something else rather than ourselves to define our self-worth. These become sources of more pain. As a result, our decisions and perceptions become fear-, shame-, and anxiety-based rather than truth-based. We do not take actions that serve us, and we do not make sustainable gains and improvements in our lives.

It is difficult for us to achieve long-term joy and happiness and have healthy, mutually beneficial relationships. Instead of joy, we seek relief. We develop neuroses and mal-adapt. We believe falsely that we do not deserve better, and so we never pursue better. We learn to settle to survive rather than to thrive. We kick into survival mode and learn not to live but to exist. In the process of avoiding our pain, we create situations that cause us more pain.

We never learn what our true self-worth and capabilities are and what we are worthy of. Instead, like Caryn, we take on false versions of ourselves, the ones we think we need to avoid pain and the self-critical versions that perpetuate the pattern of pain. We never learn to access and rely on our own strength; we readily give up our power to emotional manipulators. We become dependent on others not only to define our self-worth but also to alleviate the pain they inflict on us with their betrayal.

We never learn to be who we were put on this earth to be. We never learn the skills and coping mechanisms commensurate with our real needs to care for ourselves and build and sustain our self-esteem, self-respect, and self-power. We become wounded, pain-seeking, and pain-avoiding versions of ourselves who do not and cannot provide the emotional nourishment we need to thrive.

We become emotionally deprived and emotionally exhausted. We become prisoners to our emotions, and so we continue to suffer. We react to what others do to avoid pain; we never simply enjoy life based on what we want to do, are confident we can achieve, and believe we deserve.

Our belief systems become skewed, and our self-compassion, self-esteem, self-worth, self-love, self-respect, and self-esteem suffer. We are not our authentic selves. Our actions originate from others' expectations and needs, and from our internalized ideal of how we should be. We see other people or things as the cause and/or solution to our problems.

We learn to settle in our choice of job, career, finances, goals, and partner to serve the false version of ourselves we show to the world rather than the authentic person we really are. We self-medicate to alleviate the internal pain, shame, and self-loathing. Prolonged self-alienation, neglect of our needs, and shame frequently lead to emotional fatigue and depression.

Manipulators, narcissists, bullies, and psychopaths who cannot generate their own energy and who are experts on our vulnerabilities target us and feed off the power that we readily release to them. Some of us become abusers ourselves or passive aggressors. Some become addicted to toxic pain, drugs, and alcohol. We teach these false and self-destructive thinking patterns to our children. This is how intergenerational abuse, suffering, pain, addiction, and trauma are perpetuated.

Our lives become a vicious cycle of returning to a state of pain that we believe falsely we are deserving of and are powerless to address. We feel trapped, bringing us more angst and pain. We become addicted to pain that originated in wounds from childhood abuse. Our beliefs, in essence, become a self-fulfilling prophecy.

The good news is that we can replace the lies with truth—the real truth—to turn this unnecessary addictive cycle into a victorious one. This takes hard work, courage, and turning compassion inward. Healing requires self-focus as well as compassion, a total shift in thinking that you are not accustomed to and probably have been punished for in the past. I will caution you that this will most likely feel very uncomfortable at first but, in time, will get easier and easier. And as it does, you will become less reactive and more responsive to outside influences. You will be lots more confident in your strength and ability to consciously choose your responses to situations with due consideration for others rather than unconsciously reacting in unhealthy ways that do not serve you and keep you on the pain merry-go-round.

## Healing Lesson 2:
## It Is Never about the Other Person

Betrayal is one of the most painful human experiences. The victim's response is shame, internal pain, self-loathing, trauma, and fear. We translate that into the false belief that something is wrong with us. But there is nothing wrong with us! There never was. We did not do anything wrong. Being who we are is not wrong. Our love was real. Our trust was real. Theirs was not. We were victims.

Our attackers are character-flawed, disordered. We were betrayed because we trusted abusers, manipulators, and untrustworthy broken people. They betrayed us. We were betrayed because that is what betrayers do. It was not personal in that sense. Our attackers targeted us because they are experts on homing in on people with our vulnerabilities.

They need people with our vulnerabilities so that their manipulation tactics will be successful, so that they will win the challenge and the ultimate prize: our energy, attention, and adulation. Before you and me, there were many, and after us, there will be many more. We did not ask to be victimized, but we played a role in the abuse that we need to accept.

We were betrayed because we were vulnerable. Many of us are empaths—highly sensitive natural healers, compassionate people with high emotional intelligence. We did not learn to use our compassion and trust responsibly; we depended on untrustworthy people to define our self-worth. Our emotional vulnerabilities make us complicit in our own abuse by keeping us susceptible to abusers who preyed on us and kept us addicted to pain. This truth can be very painful, and yet it's life-changing. It will change your life forever and for the better. When we know better and that we are worthy of the knowledge, we do better.

Anger, resentment, and revenge will not heal us. Self-avoidance will not heal us. Taking responsibility and accepting without judgment will. Narcissistic abuse expert Melanie Tonia cautions us frequently that focusing too much on our abusers rather than on our healing and the role we play in our abuse can keep us trapped and prevent our recovery.

One of the most difficult lessons I learned was that I was vulnerable to attacks by manipulators and bullies. I felt threatened by them and believed I was not safe. I became fearful and resentful. My fear drove me to overestimate the harm from them and underestimate my ability to deal with them. I felt defenseless. I became hypervigilant in my attempts to avoid shame and pain as I waited for their attacks. I became hyperreactive to attacks that I was sure would come and did come. I became intolerant, which did not serve me.

In the process, I gave up my power to emotional vampires who continued to target me. Trying to avoid perceived threats kept me trapped with the people and events that triggered my fears and caused me pain. I remained a victim of the emotional vampires because I thought like a victim. I was trapped by my own fears. I became emotionally fatigued. Focusing on them rather than myself kept me from healing.

So I put on my big-girl britches and, little by little, took on and challenged my fears and my false sense of powerlessness, replacing them with courage and self-assurance. I took my power back as I came into my own truth and accepted what I could change as well as what I could not. I accepted what happened to me, took responsibility for the role I played, and shifted my thinking from that of a victim to one who wanted to take her power back, detach from and defuse the abusers, and thrive. I took action!

I adapted by turning the irrational fear and hypervigilance into compassion and tolerance. I turned that wasted fear-driven energy to the source of that fear within myself and not only challenged and released it but replaced it with self-knowledge, self-power, self-respect, and self-love. I honed my ability to identify and cope with evil people. Instead of focusing my energy on them, I shifted my attention to me and my self-worth and abilities. I protected my personal boundaries because I know and believe I am worth it.

My fear of aggressors became pity for the powerless annoyances they are. In the process, my self-esteem and self-respect soared, and I took my power back. I chose not to give my power to powerless emotional vampires and to protect my personal boundaries and honor my personal rights and authority because I know I deserve respect.

I taught my daughter the same. In the process, my daughter healed through me and thrived. It is never about the other person, folks. My dear friend Jim Upshaw told me that years ago, and I never forgot the message. Now I know the true meaning. Now I never forget the lesson.

**Healing Lesson 3:
The Only Person You Are Here to Serve Is Your Authentic Self**

When you serve your authentic self, your decisions and actions fulfill your legitimate emotional needs. You know you can rely on yourself for your safety. All of life's pieces fall into place, since the core of your being is truth-based and authentically you.

In healing, we learn to become our authentic selves—and to stop seeking approval of our worth from others. Healing is a learning process. Through asking the right questions and seeking and finding truthful answers in a safe and trusting environment, we learn to turn our compassion and courage inward to support shifts in our thinking that lead to long-term emotional health and happiness.

We learn to befriend ourselves (who we long ago abandoned) by accepting our powerlessness, committing to our healing, challenging our thoughts, releasing our fear and shame, and incrementally taking our power back as we lift up our thinking and discover and honor our real selves and our personal divinity.

In the healing process, we regain our self-trust, self-power, self-respect, and self-esteem. We learn what our true value is to ourselves. We learn to rely on and trust internal emotional cues that have been recalibrated with our personal truth and core beliefs.

Oh, of course, we must get cues from our environment and from others who have our best interests at heart. We also become better able to recognize those who do not. But we now can readily use those cues to gauge where we are and to tweak our internal truth-seeking filters based on our choices and their outcomes. In healing, we learn the following:

- to accept ourselves warts and all as enough, perfect in our being without self-criticism and fault-finding judgment
- to live with vitality, courage, and self-respect
- to think like winners, not settlers
- to formulate opinions and values that are our own
- to take informed risks and make decisions based on our own internal cues, emotions, and values
- to take ourselves back, to re-own ourselves
- to do what we want and need to do rather than what others expect of us
- to care for ourselves and respect our and others' personal rights and authority
- to use our compassion for ourselves and others responsibly
- to become resilient and bounce back quickly from setbacks
- to thought-correct and course-correct when we need to

We learn who we really are and to love ourselves. We become fully integrated people of integrity whose thoughts, actions, and beliefs align. Our healing allows us to be the best version of ourselves. It is the best demonstration of self-love we could give ourselves. And in that newfound truth, we thrive.

## Healing Lesson 4:
## We Cannot Achieve Goals at the Same Level of Thinking That Prevents Us from Achieving Them

Our human minds are wired for setting and achieving goals. We are happiest when we are not only achieving goals but setting them as well. We define who we are, who we *really* are by what we do and what we believe we are able to achieve and are worthy of. This is our self-worth. This is what we know to be true about ourselves. It is our personal truth. It is how we define our authentic selves.

As we achieve our goals, our self-worth is validated and our beliefs in our abilities are renewed. Self-help guru Denis Waitley refers to this as the "victor's circle." We gain self-respect as we validate and take back our power. In this, we create and build our authenticity. This is how we achieve happiness, success, contentment, and love. Dustin Wax, in "The Science of Setting Goals," notes that when setting a goal we invest ourselves in the target as if we'd already accomplished it. (See discussion and tips for setting and achieving goals in chapter 5.)

High self-esteem is a sign of emotional health. Emotionally healthy people are not dependent on validation from others. Once their souls are nourished, they feel complete, happy, content, valued. They know how being liked, loved, and desired makes them feel. They set and achieve goals in the belief that they are worthy of the outcome.

Victims of abuse, on the other hand, abandon themselves and have exaggerated feelings of self-loathing and shame. Their personal self-worth and self-respect suffer. Their lives are heavily based on avoiding pain and shame. They feel helpless to their emotions rather than trusting those emotions to drive them to action. They rarely set goals that serve them and bring them personal joy.

When your soul is not nourished or is depleted by abuse, overwork, and invalidation, you feel trapped and become unhappy, emotionally fatigued, depressed, sad, and traumatized. When your soul is routinely starved, you also run the risk of the following three things:

1. Believing falsely that you are the source of your pain and discomfort
2. Blaming something or someone else for your pain and discomfort
3. Feeling unsafe in your own body

All of these cause additional pain and stop you from setting goals and taking actions that nurture you and sustain your joy.

The brain cannot process two opposing thoughts at one time. When our thinking becomes pain-avoiding rather than joy-seeking, we focus on avoiding pain. We give up our inalienable right to happiness. We do not feel safe in our own bodies; we abandon ourselves, give our power away, and end up letting others who do not have our best interests at heart define our self-worth. We settle for meeting expectations others have set for us that bring us more pain and do not nourish our souls. As a result, our self-esteem and self-respect plummet.

So start now to replace those lies with your personal truth. Heal and take your power back. Turn the pain cycle into the victor's circle. Live the life you were put on this earth to live. You are worth it!

**Healing Lesson 5:
Abusers Find Us, We Do Not Find Them.**

The relationship between a chronic abuser and his or her victim is similar to the one between a parasite and its host, or a predator and its prey. Abusers seek out targets they can take energy from that the abusers cannot generate on their own. They seek out and find us because they are experts on our emotional vulnerabilities. They know how our conscience works, how to push our vulnerability buttons, and how to pursue us aggressively. They play on our neuroses and our emotional weaknesses—including exaggerated compassion, shame, and conscientiousness and our fear of abandonment—to win.

Abusers also play on therapists' weaknesses and pretend to go along with the program and say what therapists want to hear. Dr. George K. Simon explains in *Character Disturbance: The Phenomenon of Our Age* that "all their manipulation tactics effectively tap into our vulnerabilities … not only do they know how neurotics think, they know how traditionally-oriented therapists think."

Winning, to them, is taking from us what they need or whatever suits them—so it could be anything, including our confidence, attention, adulation, body—and sadistically witnessing our suffering. They use our weaknesses masterfully against us. In fact, they bank on and rely on our weaknesses to survive. Because of our pain-based thinking, we readily surrender our power. We become unknowingly complicit in our own abuse.

If your abuser is a loved one who is also a narcissist or a psychopath, your love may have been real but their professed love most likely was not. They manipulated you to acquire all the benefits of a healthy relationship but chose not to put in any of the effort required to sustain one. This open acknowledgment of love betrayal delivers much pain and shame. It can be very hard to accept and deal with in your early stages of healing, but addressing this is critical to your long-term well-being. Like any loss or betrayal, however, we mourn it during healing. The pain subsides as we learn to forgive and accept ourselves compassionately without judgment.

Understanding why abusers target us and why we stay can be fundamental to this process. The following are some truths about abusers and why they target us:

- They are abusers, personality disordered, and/or covert aggressive manipulators, and this is just what they do to survive.
- They cannot generate their own power or self-worth.
- They envy us pathologically.
- They need people with our vulnerabilities for their manipulation to be effective.
- We make good trophy mates or spouses.
- We provide the best long-lasting ego supply to fill the gaps in their broken psyches.
- We are compassionate.
- We are conscientious and hard-working.
- We are self-sacrificing.
- We are emotionally resilient.
- We have strong codependency issues and are dependent on others to define our worth.

We go along with it and stay as long as we do because of the following:

- We suffer from neuroses that make us vulnerable to their manipulation and put us in a reactive defensive mode to avoid pain.
- We long for love.
- We believe falsely based on childhood abuse that we are unlovable and must suffer and self sacrifice in love.

- We suffered trauma and shame from this relationship and/or at some time in our past from someone we trusted who betrayed us: a parent, boss, friend, relative.
- We are trauma (betrayal) addicted (bonded).
- We are empaths, natural healers, overly compassionate, and emotionally intuitive and have not learned how to use our compassion responsibly.
- We have low self-esteem and strong codependency tendencies—an unhealthy emotional dependence on others to define our worth.
- We are empaths and codependents.

Dr. Jane and Tim McGregor, authors of *The Empathy Trap: Understanding Antisocial Personalities*, reported in an *Addiction Today* article, "Empathic People Are Natural Targets for Sociopaths—Protect Yourself," the results of their profound research on people who are targets of sociopaths and aided by apaths. The McGregors called those apaths or apathetic who colluded with the sociopaths and who lacked concern for or were indifferent to the targeted person. They found that a person who is naturally compassionate and empathetic is part of the 40 percent of the population who are prime targets for scapegoaters, bullies, narcissists, con artists, and sociopaths—who in turn comprise a subset of the remaining 60 percent of the population. So being a "nice" person can put you in danger.

Empaths, they explained, are ordinary people who are highly perceptive and insightful and who sense when something's not right, who respond to their gut instinct, and who take action and speak up. Like the child in "The Emperor's New Clothes," they will tell the truth and expose lies and wrongdoing—which is exactly what makes them a target for scapegoaters, bullies, narcissists, and sociopaths who are driven by exaggerated envy and fear of shame, lack of compassion, and an inability to self-soothe.

The McGregors noted that in the 1990s, researchers suggested a positive relationship between empathy and emotional intelligence and that since then, that term has been used interchangeably with *emotional literacy*. What this means is that empaths have the ability to understand their own emotions, to listen to other people and empathize with their emotions, to express emotions productively, and to handle their emotions in such a way as to improve their personal power.

The McGregors found that people are often attracted to empaths because of their compassionate nature and sensitivity to the emotional distress of others. Conversely, empaths have trouble comprehending a closed mind and a lack of compassion in others. This is a limitation that empathetic "nice" people have and that empaths need to bring into their level of awareness.

An inability to see the bad in others significantly enhances vulnerability to attacks from emotional vampires throughout their lives. Empaths can be targeted easily by the ones who perceive them as a threat—the scapegoaters, bullies, narcissists, and sociopaths who enlist other uncompassionate and apathetic people in wrongdoing. So in actuality, abused children and adults can be some of the nicest people in the world.

This is crazy-making, folks, and it is the heart of scapegoating and abuse in families. In my opinion, it is one of the main causes of evil in society today. The number-one reason people seek counseling is because they were abused as a child—including being scapegoated—and suffer post-traumatic distress. This is psychological trauma!

Empaths use their ability to boost theirs and others' well-being and safety. Jane and Tim McGregor found it interesting how often people see empaths in problematical terms. In their research, they found that most people, the 60 percent majority, prefer the easy life and that some of us admire people who make a bold stand while others feel uneasy about them. Problems escalate for empaths, they note, when there are apaths in the vicinity and "empaths can be brought down, distressed and forced into the position of the lone fighter by the inaction of more apathetic types round them."

This is also how school and work bullying and scapegoating works. The bullies enlist the apathetic, fearful, and defenseless ones who are most likely to go along and agree that the emperor/empress is wearing new clothes. Apaths behave defenselessly because they want to avoid unpleasant or harmful circumstances (including the bully turning on them). Apathy is an avoidance strategy that contributes to abuse by proxy.

So, all you empathetic and empathic people who suffered and are recovering from abuse as a child, childhood bullying, and adult bullying—and went on to marry a narcissist or more than one narcissist—bring this into your level of awareness during your healing. Educate yourself, your children, and others on their inability to see the bad in others, the wolves in sheep's clothing. This significantly increases your vulnerability to 60 percent of people, not only narcissists, bullies, and psychopaths but also the weak apathetic ones who join these abusers or harm you further by doing nothing because they lack the heart or courage to do the right thing.

Kim Saeed, an expert on healing from narcissistic abuse, explores how narcissists prey on empaths and highly sensitive people in "Narcissists and Empaths: The Ego Dynamic." Empaths, she reports, operate predominantly from love, humility, and giving. They have a natural capacity for healing and teaching others. However, until they learn how to responsibly use those gifts, they are often taken advantage of—by romantic partners and by people in general.

She further explains that empaths have a track record of developing codependent behaviors in childhood to deal with the overwhelming unfairness in the world and to please others, which they usually carry into their adult relationships. It is easy to see, then, how empaths who were abused as children can develop exaggerated codependency issues and dependence on others to define their worth.

Saeed also points out that when an empath and a narcissist enter a relationship together, it becomes "hyper toxic and creates a magnetic, yet vibrationally dysfunctional union. The empath's soul purpose is to facilitate healing in others ... Narcissists are insatiable and incurable. The empath gives to the point of complete and utter exhaustion." Because of these natural tendencies, unaware empaths often find themselves not only being targeted by a narcissist but also staying in a relationship with a toxic personality for too long. The damage is compounded.

**Healing Lesson 6:**
**You May Be Trauma-Addicted to Your Abuser**

After we are repeatedly harmed, our fear response can go into overdrive. The trauma and pain become chemically programmed into our brain cells. The coping and defense mechanisms that should define our personal power never mature. Our perception of our personal power becomes skewed. We believe falsely that we are defenseless. We become heavily dependent on our abusers rather than ourselves to define our self-worth and power. We become dependent on them for relief from the pain. The cycle repeats with the next abusive attack. We become addicted to trauma.

It is well known that traumatized people keep choosing unreliable or abusive love partners who are similar to the original abuser who traumatized them. The victims, driven by repetition compulsion, continue to be traumatized in exploitive relationships. Exploitive relationships can create addictive trauma bonds—or what Patrick Carnes, PhD, an expert on trauma bonds, refers to as "betrayal bonds." In his book *The Betrayal Bond*, Carnes explains that when people are extremely frightened, trauma creates a biological alteration of the brain. In childhood, when immature brain functions are fully functional, we are more vulnerable and abuse can result in emotional and cognitive problems.

Carnes further describes a process that takes place when we are traumatized. The brain becomes stimulated and is flooded with chemicals called *peptides*. When the source of the fear goes away, the chemicals go away, but the person experiences cravings and can become attached to trauma. Two factors are essential in understanding traumatic experiences, according to Carnes: how far our systems are stretched and for how long. Some events happen only once or just a few times, but the impact is so great that trauma occurs. Trauma by accumulation sneaks up on its victims.

Emotional scars can be so severe that generations descended from those surviving will react in ways that reflect the original trauma. People become reactive human beings going from stimulation to impulsive action without thinking. They can react years later to earlier traumatic events, or a new traumatic event can cause the brain to make the same trauma-specific chemicals and create a new addiction to the abuser. What we perceive as extreme dangers are really triggers that open up unhealed childhood trauma wounds. People can mistake this peptide addiction for love of the abuser.

New traumatic events can also trigger our childhood feelings of powerlessness and defenselessness that keep us trapped in toxic relationships. What we perceive as being trapped is actual a child's feeling of defenselessness against our abusers. Trauma bonds cause us to grossly underestimate our ability to deal with trauma.

General signs of trauma-bonding include misplaced loyalty, inability to detach, and self-destructive denial. Specific signs of the presence of the betrayal bond defined by Carnes include the following:

- You long for your abuser.
- Everyone around you is having negative reactions so strong you are covering up, defending, or explaining the relationship.
- There is a constant pattern of abuse, and you continue to expect the abuser to follow through anyway.
- There are repetitive, destructive fights that nobody wins.
- Others are horrified by something that has happened to you, and you are not.
- You obsess about showing others that they are wrong about the abuse and your relationship.
- You feel loyal to someone even though that person harbors secrets that are damaging to others.
- You move closer to someone who is destructive with the desire of converting them to a non-abuser.
- Someone's talents, charisma, or contributions cause you to overlook destructive, exploitive, or degrading acts.
- You cannot detach from someone even though you do not trust, like, or care for the person.
- You miss a relationship even to the point of nostalgia and longing, although it was so awful it almost destroyed you.
- Extraordinary demands are placed on you to measure up as a way to cover up your exploitation.
- You keep secret someone's destructive behavior because of all of the good that person has done or the importance of that individual's position or career.
- The history of your relationship is about contracts or promises that have been broken, which you overlook.

Notice that all these characteristics involve exploitation of trust or power or both. They all can result in a bond with a person who is dangerous and exploitive.

Professional therapists can be so focused on a client's emotional wounds, neuroses, and pain that they overlook the trauma bonds that remain. If any of these signs exist, it is important for to consider trauma-bonding as a cause and to seek competent professional assistance.

## Healing Lesson 7:
## Establish Clear Goals with the Strongest Emphasis on Emotional Freedom and Health Rather Than Money, Material Possessions, or Revenge

Many abusers will fight to win. They will attempt to destroy you and your reputation, ensuring you are left with no or few resources. They may even go so far as to ensure your custody rights are revoked. In their mind, you must always lose, and they will aggressively pursue that goal. Your choice to move on and stop supplying energy to them may also incur their wrath. This is when you must appeal to your creative intelligence and strategic skills and focus on your goals. It can be very challenging but is most valuable.

Remember that money and material possessions are not indicators of success or high self-esteem. They can be regained and earned more quickly than your emotional health can be restored. Money generally is meaningless if you are emotionally unhealthy and suffering. Your depleted self-esteem will impact your ability to recover financially, so the sooner you heal the better.

In addition, revenge and benefit are not synonymous. Do not seek revenge or ever go after your abuser—or anyone, for that matter. Revenge is directing your feelings of powerlessness and fear toward your abuser, but you are still transferring your power to that person, continuing the abuse, and hampering your healing and recovery. The best type of revenge is your and your children's personal and emotional healing. In the process, you take away energy and power from the abuser. When you stop giving your power away, you can redirect it to your own and your children's recovery and well-being.

I know many people who waived hundreds of thousands of dollars of child support they were legally entitled to, since it would have kept them connected to someone they wanted to move away from. This enabled them to stealthily level the playing field, tip the scales in their favor, and minimize conflict and harm to themselves and their children. The exes, in turn, backed off. This supported the goal of emotional freedom and minimized the impact to other financial resources that they knew would benefit them more in the long term.

The following tips and facts can help you maintain your focus on attaining your emotional goals:

- Stay calm and remind yourself of your emotional healing and freedom goals even when your anger buttons are pushed. Breathe in slowly as you think good thoughts and breath out the feelings of resentment, anger, and revenge.
- Be clear that your motives during required interactions with your abuser, such as those mandated by the court or in support of your children's care, are based solely on what benefits you and your children. Give up the scorned-victim mentality.
- Most abusers are energy vampires who lack self-soothing and self-coping abilities. They cannot create their own healing energy; they need to feed off of others' energy for their personal gain and to fill the gaps in their psyches.
- Abusers get power from your negative energy. This keeps them on the offensive to continue to defeat you and take your power away.
- Use your compassion and emotional intelligence to your advantage. Play off the abuser's predictable reactions and moods. Gauge mood and meter your actions accordingly. Be careful not to overdo it. Act commensurate with what you want to achieve. Be creative. Think outside the box.

- Only interact with abusers on days when things are going their way, when they are the most malleable. Otherwise, have *no* contact with them. Remember that on their off days, they will transfer their wrath to you the way they did in the past. The objective is to minimize harm and maximize benefits, not cause you further harm that can hinder your healing.
- Avoid a court battle at all costs. Do not arbitrarily take action just because your attorney or friends tell you to. Never take punitive actions, or actions that even appear punitive. Many abusers are personality disordered. They are predictable but complex and hate to be challenged, exposed, or ashamed—and they will fight to the death to avoid all of these. They must win at all costs. They can be vicious and ruthless in their attacks, including pathologically lying about your inadequacy as a parent or your mental state. Play nice in the sandbox to tip the scales in your favor. Remember your goal. Be creative. A gutsy friend told her husband that legally having joint custody would be a burden on him that he did not deserve and that he could see his son whenever he wanted. This was true, and she ended up with the full legal custody that was in her son's best interest. She never prevented her ex from seeing their son. That turned out to be a few visits anyway, and he backed off since there was no battle or challenge for him to win.
- Adopt a "willing to lose a battle to win the war" attitude. Consider giving something up periodically to provide an illusion that the abuser won rather than challenge him or her. Abusers have aggressive personalities and have to win at all costs. If they win, you must lose. If they lose, you must lose. But you can tip the scales in your favor by strategically using tactics aligned with your goals.

# Chapter 3

# The Healing and Recovery Journey

Effective healing and recovery from pain addiction requires hard work, self-discipline, and action to recognize and resolve past pains, identify maladaptive coping behaviors, and develop new adaptive self-management skills that foster self-esteem and healthy relationships. Healing from pain addiction focuses on finding answers to the following fundamental questions:

- Why do I love someone who inflicts pain on me?
- Why did this happen to me?
- Why did he/she/they do this to me? Why did I let them?
- Why do abusers and manipulators target me?
- What is emotionally unhealthy? What is emotionally healthy? What does it feel like?
- What is an emotionally healthy relationship? What does it look and feel like?
- What false personal beliefs prevent me from believing I am worthy of emotionally healthy relationships? Of happiness? What keeps me in emotionally unhealthy relationships?
- What triggers my pains, shame, and fear? How do I become more proactive rather than reactive in situations I perceive as unpleasant or painful?
- How do I become less dependent on others and more on my own self to define who I am? My worth?
- How do I learn to feel safe in my own body?
- How do I learn to trust my own emotions?
- How do I become more dependent on and trusting of my own abilities to cope and self-soothe?
- What is preventing me from healing?

- What self-management skills am I lacking, and how do I acquire these?
- How can I release childhood trauma wounds?
- Who do I want to be, and what do I want to start creating now?

Answering these questions is not easy and can be quite painful for abuse survivors. It requires more than just abstinence or avoiding our pain sources by leaving our abusers.

Healing requires us to put our egos aside, reconnect with the selves we long ago abandoned, and uncover who we really are. It involves taking action and dealing with the familiar pains and fears we are comfortable with that have kept us feeling emotionally powerless and paralyzed, and made us want to seek protective cover. It challenges us to reject what is familiar, stay with whatever feelings emerge, and face the repressed pains and fears we've kept hidden. It requires courage and strength and self-empathy, qualities we most likely have never developed or rarely used.

The healing and recovery approach I endorse is the Adult Survivors of Child Abuse (ASCA) recovery program developed by the Morris Center for Healing from Child Abuse in San Francisco, California.

## The Adult Survivor of Child Abuse Recovery Program

The ASCA program, as described in the *ASCA Survivor to Thriver Manual*, is a three-stage, twenty-one-step program tailored to abuse victims' unique needs. It is designed to serve as an adjunct to traditional therapies and self-help programs.

Healing from abuse is similar to recovering from chemical, sex, and other addictions because the root causes of repeating pain cycles that drive addictive behaviors are the same. However, there are some fundamental differences related to victimization, shame, blame, and trauma that are addressed uniquely for abuse and trauma victims in the ASCA program.

Experts have also recently discovered that treating addictions is more successful if the trauma wounds are addressed in addition to the obvious self-esteem and other emotional issues causing the chemical addiction. So the healing and recovery strategies proposed in the ASCA program, while designed for abuse victims, can also be extremely beneficial to those recovering from chemical and other addictions who have trauma wounds.

The ASCA approach addresses these needs in three stages: remembering, mourning, and healing. In the discussion below, I add a fourth stage to address unconscious exaggerated pain wounds because I firmly believe, based on my years of research and the personal input I have received from thousands of survivors, that this is an area of healing that warrants specialized attention, resources, and assistance because it provides hidden emotional challenges and obstacles to healing and long-term health, such as those faced by victims of narcissistic abuse.

*How Does the ASCA Recovery Program Work?*

The ASCA recovery framework is a three-stage model for healing. Each stage contains seven steps, with assigned tasks and tools to support self-evaluation and incremental emotional healing and growth through that stage. As you complete each step, you learn to trust your emotions without fear and build skills to enable you to take effective action. You can use the steps as milestone markers to gauge your progress in your healing journey.

The ASCA framework uses a flexible phased healing approach called StepWork. StepWork allows you to choose which steps apply to you, concentrate on one particular step or milestone, and work at your own pace to accommodate your learning style and personal needs.

With the ASCA program, you don't have to complete the steps in any particular order. You have the freedom to jump ahead to other steps or jump back to milestones you already have reached based on new lessons or skills learned. As described in the *ASCA Survivor to Thriver Manual*, the program is designed to complement local or online ASCA meetings and your individual therapy sessions. The manual includes questions, exercises, and suggestions that can be referenced and used independently to support your self-help in your healing and recovery. Each of the three stages includes seven steps or recovery milestones.

**Stage 1: Remembering**

The remembering steps of Stage 1 relate to uncovering the truth about your childhood abuse. You must acknowledge what happened in the past before you can move forward in recovery. This becomes the foundation upon which you build your recovery. The seven steps are as follows:

1. I am in a breakthrough crisis, having gained some sense of my abuse.
2. I have determined that I was physically, sexually, or emotionally abused as a child.
3. I have made a commitment to recovery from my childhood abuse.
4. I shall re-experience each set of memories as they surface in my mind.
5. I accept that I was powerless over my abusers' actions that hold *them* responsible.
6. I can respect my shame and anger as a consequence of my abuse but shall try not to turn it against myself or others.
7. I can sense my inner child, whose efforts to survive can now be appreciated.

## Stage 2: Mourning

The mourning steps in Stage 2 focus on examining your adult behavior, connecting your present strengths and weaknesses to the abuse you suffered and the coping mechanisms you adopted, and allowing the child within to grieve the aspects of childhood that never existed for you. The seven steps are as follows:

1. I have made an inventory of the problem areas in my adult life.
2. I have identified the parts of myself connected to self-sabotage.
3. I can control my anger and find healthy outlets for my aggression.
4. I can identify faulty beliefs and distorted perceptions in myself and others.
5. I am facing my shame and developing self-compassion.
6. I accept that I have the right to be who I want to be and live the way I want to live.
7. I am able to grieve my childhood and mourn the loss of those who failed me.

## Stage 3: Healing

The healing steps in Stage 3 involve consolidating your new, healthier feelings and behaviors, your feelings about the abuse, and your adult goals into a new sense of self and then going out and practicing this new self in the world.

1. I am entitled to take the initiative to share in life's riches.
2. I am strengthening the healthy parts of myself, adding to my self-esteem.
3. I can make necessary changes in my behavior and relationships at home and at work.

4. I have resolved the abuse with my offenders to the extent that is acceptable to me.
5. I hold my own meaning about the abuse that releases me from the legacy of the past.
6. I see myself as a thriver in all aspects of life—love, work, parenting, and play.
7. I am resolved in the reunion of my new self and eternal soul.

## Stage 4: Recovering from Traumatic Stress, Toxic Shame, and Toxic Grief

I've added a fourth stage to the program to highlight and address exaggerated unconscious trauma and painful emotions that warrant specialized attention, resources, and assistance. These not-so-obvious emotional challenges can provide the biggest obstacles to healing. While shame and grief are addressed in Stages 1 and 2, Stage 4 focuses on addressing and releasing the sources of our deep-seated chronic pain, including traumatic stress and toxic shame and grief. These are faced by victims of narcissistic abuse as adults or as children. The seven steps are as follows:

1. I embrace my toxic painful emotions and do not fear them.
2. When I fall short, I take responsibility for the part I played and seek help to take action and achieve my goals.
3. I have replaced my victim thinking with victor thinking.
4. I have grieved my childhood and adult relationships and mourned the loss of loved ones who betrayed me.
5. I can identify sources, triggers, and early warning signs of my pain and make choices to address them before they escalate.

6. I replaced the fear and avoidance of my emotions with self-acceptance and self-compassion, and my newfound autonomy keeps me accountable to my healing goals and fuels my new life.
7. I have taken my power back and feel safe in my body.

**Where Do I Start?**

Starting recovery can be the most daunting part of your journey. Our search for answers can be brought on by personal catastrophes or crises—such as losing a loved one or being abandoned or betrayed by someone we intimately trusted—which have opened repressed trauma wounds. Others who are emotionally exhausted may just be ready to heal. Whichever the case, you are seeking answers (the real truth, not the glittered version) because your actions and decisions do not and have not served you well.

Healing starts with turning your compassion and care inward and respecting your emotions. It requires us to develop empathy for the wounded child within that will inspire us to commit to ourselves and to our healing. It also requires us to give up resentment and feelings of revenge toward our attackers and to take responsibility for the roles we played in our continued abuse.

According to the ASCA, as a child, you developed formidable psychological defenses to protect yourself against abuse, and you probably continued to rely on these rigid defenses well into adulthood, until they no longer worked for you. This is where you may be now. However, distorted thinking patterns, maladaptive coping mechanisms, and neuroses can hamper your recovery. Your ego has served a protective purpose, shielding you from your real pain, hiding those parts you don't want the world to see and showing to others what you think they should see. Your inner critic repeats harmful childhood lies that perpetuate childhood-based pains, fears, and feelings of hopelessness.

Abuse victims lack the self-compassion and self-empathy required for healing and self-evaluation. They have learned to criticize and reject rather than trust, respect, honor, and respond kindly to emotions that play an important role in emotional health. Chronic emotional pain can trigger anxiety, depression, and panic attacks.

Victims can also deny or suppress painful memories to protect themselves from psychological pain. They may be shame-ridden and unable to accept their roles in the abuse. Skilled recovery counselor Glynis Sherwood explains that respecting our emotions is important to our recovery because emotions tell us whether our beliefs and experiences are positive, neutral, or negative. They are essential to making informed choices about whether to stay the course or change our thoughts or the situation we find ourselves in for the better. Healthy emotions add depth and passion to life.

Healing also requires development of goals and timelines for achieving them. We may have difficulty setting goals and taking action if we do not know what emotional health is and what it feels like. See Healing Lessons 1 through 7 in chapter 2 to help you challenge beliefs that can hamper your healing. "My Personal Commitment to the Healing and Life I Deserve" and "A Look into the Future of Your Healing Journey" in appendix 1 and inspirational quotes in appendix 2 can also serve as healing motivators and catalysts.

Self-evaluation is important during healing because we are able to assess what we know, what we do not know, and what we would like to know. We can then begin to recognize our own strengths and vulnerabilities, shift our faulty thinking, set goals that we know we deserve and can attain with the new knowledge we acquire about ourselves, and achieve goals with the emotional strength we regain.

However, self-evaluation can be especially difficult for adult victims of child abuse who have developed an aversion to self-care because they were punished for it in the past. Even basic needs can trigger feelings of panic, self-loathing, and hopelessness. Our shame may also be so exaggerated, and we may be so comfortable in our self-criticism that we become hypercritical or consumed with blame during our self-evaluation, when our emotions can be heightened. When pain-based emotions are removed from the situation, it's like being exposed at the end of a theatre production when the lights are turned on.

This courageous surrender of control allows us to turn our lives over to our own power, tap into our own strength, and learn to trust our emotions and act on them. As Darlene Lancer explains so eloquently in *Conquering Shame and Codependency*, "the objective is to voluntarily experience the emptiness that occurs by *intentionally not trying to escape despair*."

Guided exercises from competent coaches and therapists can help you develop empathy and compassion, as well as the focus on and accountability to your goals that are needed to facilitate your healing and recovery. Self-help support communities like Yourlifelifter (https://www.facebook.com/yourlifelifter and https://yourlifelifter.wordpress.com) can be instrumental at this juncture and provide free resources, information, and unconditional compassion to those needing help. They can also provide a community of belonging, a "family," that may not be available to victims or was not available to them growing up. These communities offer relief and safe haven from the isolation, loneliness, insecurity, fear, blame, and shame victims face. Seeing others honestly sharing their pain and similar stories in a mutually supportive setting frees you to do the same and helps to improve your self-esteem.

Trying to initiate and proceed with recovery when your daily life is unstable can also set you up for failure. The ASCA notes that many abuse survivors function in reactive "crisis mode" because of irregularity, unpredictability, and inconsistency in their lives caused by their ongoing internal chaos. Each new crisis consumes precious energy and attention that, after years, can lead to discouragement, helplessness, and hopelessness. Recovery, then, is unlikely until you bring some order to your life. The ASCA hot-spots checklist in Appendix 1 can help you identify, rank, and address the issues that may be diverting energy from your recovery efforts.

# Chapter 4

# Recovering from Traumatic Stress and Toxic Shame and Grief

Shame, sadness, and grief are normal, unconscious, protective human emotions that help us put on the brakes by taking danger cues from our external environment. They help us cope and adapt, and they support our growth and survival. However, victims of abuse can end up with too high a level of these pain emotions repressed in their memories. Emotional responses become exaggerated from repetitive abuse that overstresses them and causes them to malfunction.

Narcissistic abuse recovery expert Melanie Tonia Evans clarifies in "The Difference Between the Inner Child and the Ego" that "the most powerful belief systems are created by the intensity of emotional charge that was attached to them so the most painful childhood events (that you may not remember now because you submerged them long ago) are the ones setting up your future destiny without you realizing it. Belief systems work like this—they generate with life the evidence of the belief."

So what were intended as protective adaptive emotions can become toxic in adult survivors of childhood abuse. Abuse victims end up with too many of these protective emotions locked in their body and subconscious, keeping them trapped in destructive thought patterns and relationships. They are, in effect, traumatic to a child ill-equipped to deal with the pain.

Pain and trauma therapist Glynis Sherwood further explains in "Stop the Struggle: Five Steps to Breaking Free from Chronic Emotional Pain" that:

Trauma is a complicated form of anxiety that gets locked in our bodies and our minds in response to events that are so overwhelming that the mind attempts to bury them in the subconscious. It's a creative solution that unfortunately doesn't work since repressed memories can't heal and continue to resurface in response to triggers in the present, such as stress or situations, people or even odors or sounds that are reminiscent of the original trauma.

Dr. Bessel van der Kolk, a leading world authority on post-traumatic stress disorder (PTSD), adds in *The Body Keeps the Score* that:

> When you are traumatized your motion is paralyzed. A victim of violence almost invariably has been trapped, pinned down or unable to move. Later, if there is a perceived threat, the body reacts as if it has to move but it once again feels helpless and paralyzed, prevented from being able to act effectively. All the chemicals are released to engage in action but the body doesn't know how to move. Their challenge is that after confrontation with physical helplessness, it is essential to engage in taking effective action.

So trauma and shame can keep us codependent and addicted to those who are destructive to us, similar to addictions to drugs and alcohol, and to abusive and emotionally unhealthy situations, beliefs, jobs, and habits. We can long for our abusers and even protect them because we embrace trauma and pain that we feel we have more control over than, for example, our solitude that pushes abandonment buttons.

Early warning signs of trauma can include feeling spaced out, numb, and disconnected from others or your surroundings. Traumatic memories may appear as flashbacks or as nightmares that include visions of the original event and create intense fear and disorientation. When traumatic pain—including exaggerated shame and prolonged grief—are triggered, we become hypervigilant, reactive, aggressive, and sensitive to criticism. We feel self-loathing, anger, fear, anxiety, and depression. These in turn can jump-start self-criticism and aggression that grow out of our deep-seated feelings of powerlessness.

These emotional drugs distort our reality and keep us in harmful relationships and situations that put us at continued risk. Trauma and pain become chemically programmed into our brain cells and repressed in our subconscious memories, causing unconscious wounds that we cannot readily access and heal. Our own bodies betray us by failing to guarantee safety. We become afraid of our own feelings that bring us chronic fear, pain, or helplessness. Repressing our feelings only causes us more pain.

Toxic pain becomes a normal emotion for victims of abuse and can become so extreme that it causes us to turn over our personal power to others who do not have our best interests at heart and who continue to push our pain triggers. We go back to the abusers or turn to legal or illegal medications or alcohol or other harmful sources for relief. This is how pain, chemical, and other addictions are perpetuated.

Trauma from childhood and adult abuse wire our brains for fear that can manifest as PTSD and trauma addictions. Traumatic memory cannot distinguish between a past threat and safety, so victims of PTSD suffer heightened fear and powerlessness in the face of sounds, memories, or people that trigger the trauma. Traumatized individuals can also keep choosing abusive partners who trigger familiar but harmful emotions and reopen old wounds.

Exploitive relationships can themselves create addictive trauma bonds. As mentioned in Healing Lesson 6 in chapter 2, after we are repeatedly harmed in relationships, we can become trauma-addicted. We become dependent on our abusers for relief from pain. The cycle repeats with the next abusive attack. Once the emotional emergency passes, we lay in wait for the next trigger and the next relief. If you are experiencing any signs listed in Healing Lesson 6, it is important to consider trauma-bonding as a cause and to seek professional assistance.

Similarly, our shame and grief responses can become exaggerated from repetitive abuse that overstresses what should be protective emotions and causes them to malfunction. We become addicted to the pain and surrender our self-esteem and power to whatever or whomever triggers the overstressed trauma-, shame-, and grief-filled emotions; we remain captive to our own irrational beliefs. Staying subconsciously trapped by repressed pain and fear (our neuroses) can keep us vulnerable to narcissists and other covert aggressors who hunt for and feed off of our vulnerabilities. Read more in Healing Lesson 5 in chapter 2.

After leaving her narcissistic abuser, one of my clients wrote to me desperately asking for help and confessing that

> all it takes is one contact, a text message through my adult son's phone number from my ex and my mind takes on his voice and the recriminations start playing over and over in my head. It is so hard to shut that voice up and it can drag me to the bottom of the hopeless pit very quickly. I feel like I'm crazy not being able to stop it … My instinct to panic and run away and take undue blame and shame are affecting my work and life.

Therapists can focus so much on our external symptoms—such as feelings of resentment and the need for revenge—that they miss the toxic and subconscious grief, trauma, and shame that are keeping us addicted to our abusers and powerless to our pain. There are self-help strategies and alternative therapies that can help you feel less overwhelmed. See "Tips for Dealing with Trauma, Shame, and Grief" later in this chapter and in appendix 1.

**Toxic Shame and Toxic Grief Can Be Our Biggest Traps**

As discussed in chapter 1, the primary pain we feel from abuse is the shame of betrayal. Shame is the part of us we can't face because it is so intolerable. Webster defines shame as the painful feeling arising from the consciousness of something dishonorable, improper, and ridiculous done by oneself or another. It is a kind of injury to one's pride or self-respect.

Shame guru Darlene Lancer explains that toxic shame gets internalized as a state of bring that becomes part of a package of self-blame, self-loathing, bad feelings, self-destructive thoughts, and self-sabotaging behaviors. Too much shame leads to the kind of flawed, defective existence we believe we deserve. Too much shame can make us targets of toxic manipulators, keep us powerless to them, and trigger our anger at inappropriate times. In a *PsychCentral* article on "Understanding Shame," Karyn Hall writes that

> shame involves feelings of helplessness, incompetence, inferiority, and powerlessness and generates a desire to escape or avoid contact with others as well as conceal deficiencies. Shame means pretending, wearing a mask to prevent others from realizing how flawed the person is. Shame can be a constant, nagging sense of unworthiness, of being flawed. The constant fear of being "found out" is exhausting.

Shame can keep us addicted to our abusers where we believe the pain is more controllable than the worthlessness we feel powerless over when we're alone. We become prisoners to our shame, which causes us to become unknowingly complicit in our abuse. Chronic shame addictions keep us trapped in harmful relationships. What we perceive as dangers are really triggers that are pushing our wounded inner child's pain buttons; what we perceive as powerlessness and hopelessness are really our wounded inner child's feeling of defenselessness.

Note that Stages 1 and 2 in the ASCA abuse recovery program discussed in chapter 3 include exercises and steps to address your shame and replace it with compassion and self-respect. It is also important in recovery to learn to distinguish between guilt, which can motivate healing, and shame, which can hinder it. Michael A. Wright, PhD, explains in "Accountability Is Not Shame, but Guilt Can Be Motivating" that "the problem with shame is that it obscures the desired goals in favor of self-protection or saving-face goals." According to Wright:

> In every situation in which you fall short of a goal, you are faced with either guilt or shame. Simply put, guilt is actively taking responsibility. Shame is passively having blame assigned to you. Guilt causes you to assess what you have done wrong and take steps to correct your behaviors. Shame, on the other hand, causes you to seek cover. If you do not like conflict, you hide with denial and avoidance. If you are more comfortable with conflict, you engage attempting to refocus the light of conviction on something other than your behaviors and your choices.

Chronic or prolonged grief can also result from unresolved childhood abuse and from feelings of abandonment. While grief is a normal response to any significant loss, it can get stuck if the grieving person is having issues accepting or adjusting to the loss. Stage 2 in the ASCA abuse recovery program includes steps and exercises to allow you to grieve the aspects of childhood that never existed for you.

Grief, like trauma and shame, can be triggered unexpectedly by losses or disappointments in adulthood—such as breakups, divorce, or alienation from a dysfunctional family. In a *Huffington Post* interview with Allen Francis, "When Good Grief Goes Bad," renowned grief expert Dr. Holly Prigerson explains the difference between healthy and unhealthy grief as follows:

> Grief is a normal process of accommodating to the new life that has to be lived in the absence of a loved one. Most of the bereaved manage to get through the worst of their grief and continue to function and to find meaning in life. Normal grief differs from prolonged grief in that it is not as intense, persistent, disabling and life-altering and is not experienced as a severe threat to the survivor's identity, sense of self-worth, feelings of security, safety or hopes for future happiness. Although normal grief remains with the bereaved person far into the future, its ability to disrupt the survivor's life dissipates with time. This is "good grief" in the sense that it runs a natural course and is part of an adaptive process.

The good news is that through healing, adult survivors of childhood abuse can convert these maladaptive pain-based emotions of traumatic stress, shame, and grief into adaptive ones. You can learn to be more aware of pain triggers and make choices that will interrupt the pain cycle and allow you to cope better. In your healing journey, you learn through observation and challenging your thoughts that the exaggerated trauma, shame, and grief that have controlled your life and limited your emotional growth are merely mental constructs. They are familiar but not correct.

Recurring pain symptoms are best dealt with in psychotherapy with a skilled counselor; however, you can learn personal strategies to help you feel less overwhelmed. See the following tips for dealing with traumatic stress and chronic shame and grief; they are also listed in appendix 1.

**Tips for Dealing with Trauma, Shame, and Grief**

*Tip 1: Create a Healing Mind-Set*

- Turn your compassion and tolerance toward yourself and accept your feelings and yourself—warts and all—as a valuable person.
- Educate yourself on trauma, shame, and grief, and their debilitating effects.
- Learn to identify the feelings of emotional pain, trauma, shame, and guilt as they occur in your daily life. Write in a journal about situations and relationships that trigger them. Learn to bring these events into your level of awareness and identify these triggers (see Tip 2 below).
- Challenge your emotions. Ask yourself which ones result from lack of compassion and tolerance for yourself. For example, "Even though I feel sad, I am still a caring person, able to go to work and take care of my children."
- Work on these areas as traumatic-pain trigger points and do what you can to avoid them or minimize their harmful effects.
- Get rid of toxic friends who habitually violate your trust and your personal boundaries.

- Be consistent and fair about sharing your compassion and tolerance with yourself as well as with others.
- Go first with your compassion. Learn to be tolerant of yourself first. Know when to quit, rest, and say you have had enough. This is not selfish. This is self-preservation and what emotionally healthy people do.
- Respect your own personal boundaries. Demonstrate kindness and acceptance to honor yourself. Do not violate your own personal wishes, body, trust, time, privacy, feelings, and property.
- Do not let other people violate your personal boundaries. See chapter 5 on "Building Self-Esteem and Self-Compassion."
- Stop defending your feelings, preferences, trust, time, and choices to abusers. Abusers use this as an opportunity to abuse you more and expose you to more trauma and shame. If you must respond to their sneaky insults or criticism, just say, "That's interesting. Let me think about it." Then ignore them and turn their comments into a non-issue.
- Focus on gratitude for what you have. My mother told me if you have food, a roof over your head, your health, and people who love you, you have everything. She was right.
- Avoid black-and-white thinking that focuses only on good or bad outcomes. Look at your track record.
- Refrain from complaining about what you disagree with or do not like in yourself. If you have nothing nice to say or think about yourself, don't say or think it.
- Welcome and view disagreements from trusted individuals or differences not as criticism but as motivation to learn more and become a person of integrity.
- Give yourself a break. Be careful to understand the difference between rejecting the sin and rejecting the sinner. Learn to say "who cares?" more.

- Don't judge a book by its cover. Don't rush to judgment. Refrain from developing an opinion before you get all the facts. If in doubt, ask a wise and trusted friend.
- Refrain from making yourself the brunt of jokes or laughter.
- Do not always stand in the back of the line. Allow yourself to go first sometimes.

*Tip 2: Learn Your Triggers and Early Warning Signs and Address Them before They Escalate*

- Implementing constructive solutions is where confidence and mastery come from. If you find yourself triggered into stress, anxiety, self-loathing, sadness, grief, or trauma, ask yourself "Is this a problem that I need to deal with on my own, or with the help of others or both? Does it require change or acceptance or both?"
- Acknowledge your painful feelings. This can be a challenge if you've been criticized or unsupported when experiencing difficult emotions in the past. Understanding the causes of challenging emotions helps you predict and possibly avoid these situations. From there you can make choices about how to deal with reoccurring patterns of negative thinking or interpersonal situations that can cause problems.
- Express your emotions by writing them down. It is also important to write down what happened to make you feel upset, and how you plan to deal with it.
- Identify personal strengths that can help you at this time. After all, you've survived so far and taken care of yourself, so you have a track record of landing on your feet. Let this help you develop a realistic, optimistic, caring attitude toward yourself.

- If you identify any weak areas within yourself that need strengthening, make a plan to develop more resilience. For example, if you lack confidence, you need a strategy to foster more faith in yourself. Do you need to build more personal stamina, or is it more a question of softening your attitude toward yourself?
- It may be helpful to talk about your pain and your strengths with a nonjudgmental friend, support group, or counselor who can see the abilities that you minimize and don't see in yourself.

*Tip 3: Resist the Urge to Consider Accountability to Your Healing Goals as Shame*

In "Accountability Is Not Shame, but Guilt Can Be Motivating," Michael A. Wright, PhD, gives this advice:

> When you feel you have fallen short, determine whether you are responding to guilt or shame. If you are responding to guilt you will ask, "What choices did I make that were not in line with my goals? What choices can I make now to move sustainably toward my goals?" If you are responding to shame and engaging in conflict you will exclaim, "There are many reasons why I am not achieving my goals! Few people understand my struggle."

Learn to replace your triggered shame with a healthier dose of guilt, which empowers you to take responsibility and seek help to achieve your recovery goals.

*Tip 4: Take Anger Management Classes*

Shame triggers anger, which can lead to interpersonal conflicts in addition to unnecessary angst. Anger management classes can help you compassionately identify the sources of your fears and frustrations, validate these feelings, and provide constructive coping and communication strategies to manage them before they escalate.

*Tip 5: Look at Your Track Record from Youth*

Recall people in your childhood who had something good to say about you—those who were kind to you, like teachers, clergy, neighbors, a surrogate parent, or perhaps a relative. What words did they use to describe your best qualities? How did you feel when you were around them? Revive these important people from your past by writing about them in a journal and exploring what their support meant to you, then and now.

*Tip 6: Look to a Higher Power*

If you are religious or spiritual, turn to your Higher Power or Source to cleanse you of the shame and unworthiness you feel so deeply. Religion and spiritual practice can be tremendous sources of inner sustenance and provide an ideal vision to replace the negative role models and scenarios of the past.

*Tip 7: Get Good Feedback*

Good feedback is honest, constructive, and unbiased. Share your struggles with working this step on support blogs, group therapy meetings, a wise and trusted friend, and Facebook self-help communities like Yourlifelifter, Detoxify You, and After Narcissistic Abuse.

*Tip 8: Learn the Signs of Trauma-Bonding*

As discussed in Healing Lesson 6 in chapter 2, if you have any of the symptoms of trauma-bonding, your trauma must be treated like an addiction. You are not thinking of your abuser because of love and some sort of soul-connected mystical control he or she has over you. The abuser is your drug, and the severity of the abuse has caused chemical changes in your brain that have created a trauma addiction. Please seek out professional therapy.

When we recover from addictions, we will have cravings during times of stress. This is why we think of our abusers. You're not missing that individual in the sense that you miss an abusive and dangerous predator; you miss the addiction to the cycles that individual created. The craving is what causes a relapse.

The idea is to get enough time away from the trauma source to heal our brains. This is why no contact with your abuser is warranted for our healing. You must also change situations in your life that trigger cravings. Use support systems from therapy and support groups, and change any daily habits you had with the abuser.

You need to change your thinking patterns, be very good to yourself, be kind and compassionate, and learn skills that will keep you feeling safe in the present moment. This includes traditional and alternative therapies, such as meditation, prayer, yoga, exercise, or whatever will move your thought processes away from the abuser and toward your own self-care and self-soothing. See Tips 9, 10, and 11 below.

*Tip 9: Regain Control through Rhythmical Movement*

Take classes in rhythmical movement like yoga and tango dancing to get back in charge of your body. Renowned trauma expert Dr. Bessel van der Kolk has pioneered the use of yoga as a therapy that is helping individuals work through their PTSD.

He reports in *The Body Keeps the Score: Brain, Mind, and Body in the Healing of Trauma* that the issue of self-regulation needs to be front and center in the treatment of traumatized people.

Yoga teaches those who feel trapped in their memory sensations that emotions can come to an end. It allows those suffering from traumatic stress to observe that discomfort can be tolerated until they shift into a different posture when the emotions end. Rhythmical movements help us reintegrate the personal rhythms that we lose when we are traumatized. Both teach us that there are things we can do—other than take legal or illegal medications—to quiet the brain and reintegrate not only with ourselves but also with others from whom trauma has separated us.

*Tip 10: Consider Other Alternative Therapies*

Proven effective therapies for releasing pain and trauma include hypnotherapy, Eye Movement Desensitization and Reprocessing (EMDR), Emotional Freedom Techniques based on acupressure, and the Quanta Freedom Healing system by narcissistic abuse recovery expert Melanie Tonia Evans.

*Tip 11: Seek Competent Professional Therapy*

The ASCA recommends finding a professional therapist if you are not progressing in your healing and recovery. You may be trauma-addicted or suffering from toxic traumatic stress and chronic shame and grief.

In order to resolve pain addictions, an ongoing reparative relationship with a qualified abuse therapist can help you challenge your internal self-critical dialogue and replace it with a healthier one. A therapist can also help you find words to communicate your internal feelings of powerlessness and fear, validate them, and free you from being locked inside yourself.

If you experience exaggerated shame, a competent therapist is an important ally in helping you transform the shame into self-acceptance. Talk about your shame with your therapist and share how you experienced shame in your childhood and in your life, including in your therapy sessions. With your therapist's help, identify the ways in which you keep yourself from feeling your shame by adopting a role or false self that you portray for others based on what you think is acceptable to them rather than yourself.

Share this false self with your therapist and try to understand what the role gives you that you feel you lack. This can help you hone in on shame triggers you can work to acknowledge, challenge, release, and replace with new rational beliefs and emotions that support your emotional health and well-being.

# Chapter 5

# Building Self-Esteem and Self-Compassion

As discussed in Healing Lesson 1 in chapter 2, high self-esteem is a sign of emotional health. Self-esteem exists as a consequence of the implicit judgment that every person has of his or her ability to face life's challenges, to understand and solve problems, to achieve happiness, and to be given respect. Self-esteem is a conscious decision we make about our self-worth and reflects confidence in our ability to take risks, love and be loved, protect ourselves, and achieve goals that bring us joy.

Improving our self-esteem and self-compassion is a milestone for abuse survivors who were taught to focus on pain rather than joy and even basic needs and to feel powerless over emotional discomforts. Critical to our self-esteem, then, is our ability to care for, soothe, and nurture our own selves and to turn our compassion inward, something abuse victims lack the ability to do.

Healthy self-esteem allows us to become more autonomous and look to ourselves to define our self-worth. It also allows us to protect our personal rights and authorities from boundary violators and emotional vampires and to become resilient to shame, which most abuse victims suffer from. Healthy self-esteem allows us to rely on ourselves for validation of our self-worth because we know what we are capable of doing, know we are worthy of joy, and set goals to bring ourselves joy that we are confident we can achieve. When we do not achieve our goals, we do not hunker down in shame, but we do course-correct or get advice or assistance to achieve our goals. We do not take no for an answer when it comes to achieving our goals. The role of other people is not to validate us but to complement us and share our joy. We do not need anything from them because we are self-sufficient.

People with high self-esteem are clear on their lovability and the level of respect and honor they and others deserve and expect in any relationship—be it personal, family, or employment. We choose to love or be with someone because their self-esteem and personal truth align with ours. Mutual alignment of truths—including common values, goals, and levels of integrity—is what makes people desirable, likable, lovable, and valuable to persons with high self-esteem.

People with low self-esteem, on the other hand, cannot look internally for validation of their self-worth and typically are pain-addicted from abuse, trauma, or possibly more severe psychological issues. They also have a high tendency toward codependency. Other people become sources or solutions to their pain.

**Evaluating Your Self-Esteem**

Here are some characteristics of those with high self-esteem. Which ones do you possess? Which ones do you feel you need to work on? Answering these questions can help you gauge where you are in recovery and where you need to focus and set or revisit some milestones and goals. People with a healthy level of self-esteem do the following:

- set joy-seeking goals they know they deserve and are confident in their ability to achieve
- understand well what their personal boundaries and authority are and understand their right to have theirs honored and respected
- are tolerant of other people's differences

- can work toward finding solutions and voice discontent without belittling themselves or others when challenges arise
- practice self-compassion, including self-care, self-kindness, and self-nurturance when they are in emotional pain or are distressed
- firmly believe in certain values and principles, which they are ready to defend even when finding opposition, while feeling secure enough to modify them in light of experience
- act according to what they think to be the best choice, trusting their own judgment and not feeling guilty when others do not like their choice
- refuse to judge themselves and lose time worrying excessively about what happened in the past, nor about what could happen in the future
- learn from the past and plan for the future, but live in the present intensely
- fully trust in their capacity to solve problems, not hesitating after failures and difficulties but asking others for help when needed
- consider themselves equal in dignity to others rather than inferior or superior, while accepting differences in certain talents, personal prestige, or financial standing
- understand how they are an interesting and valuable person for others, at least for those with whom they have a friendship
- resist manipulation and collaborate with others only if it seems appropriate and convenient
- admit and accept different internal feelings and drives, either positive or negative, revealing those drives to others only when they choose
- enjoy a great variety of activities
- show sensitivity to feelings and needs of others

- respect generally accepted social rules
- claim no right or desire to prosper at others' expense
- use their compassion responsibly to their and others' benefit.

Appendix 1 includes links to self-esteem tests and tools that you can use to gauge and improve your self-esteem, such as positive affirmations that replace negative harmful beliefs with ones that support unconditional acceptance. Honoring your personal boundaries, rights, and authority while setting and achieving goals that support healthy self-esteem is discussed later in this chapter.

Getting your self-esteem and compassion to healthy levels is a process, similar to teaching self-worth and confidence to a child who has been dependent on his or her parents for validation of worth and feelings. Building our self-esteem requires us to put in effort, endure trial and error, overcome fears, and take risks. It requires action.

We are adults now and can tap into personal strength we did not have as children. Our brains are elastic enough to rewire and reprogram, and so we can learn to replace the pain-seeking/avoiding thinking of a victim with the joy-seeking thinking of a victor. This is how we take our power back. This is how we take risks, love and protect ourselves, and achieve goals. This is how we thrive.

**Personal Boundaries, Rights, and Authority**

An unhealthy relationship is founded on unhealthy personal boundaries just like a healthy relationship is founded on healthy boundaries. Not honoring others' personal boundaries devalues others. It is violating their and your personal rights and power for personal gain. But allowing habitual violation of personal boundaries is a sign of low self-esteem. This giving up of your personal power to others is a common characteristic of abuse survivors.

Validation and respect by others validates our self-worth. On the other hand, invalidation and disrespect by others diminishes our self-worth and wreaks havoc with our self-esteem. It brings us emotional discomfort and pain. Honoring personal boundaries is honoring our value and divinity as human beings and respecting our right to act on and defend them.

Chronic invalidation of our emotions and feelings negates the benefits of our protective emotions and feelings. They malfunction and become toxic. This toxicity follows us from childhood to adulthood. Steven Hein, a renowned expert on emotional intelligence, reports at core.eqi.org that psychological invalidation is one of the most lethal forms of emotional abuse and kills confidence, creativity, and individuality. Constant invalidation implies we are fundamentally abnormal, and it may be one of the most significant reasons a person with high innate emotional intelligence suffers from unmet emotional needs later in life. In "Emotional Validation," he explains that

> a sensitive child, who is repeatedly invalidated becomes confused and begins to distrust his own emotions. He fails to develop confidence in and healthy use of his emotional brain—one of nature's most basic survival tools. To adapt to this unhealthy and dysfunctional environment, the working relationship between his thoughts and feelings becomes twisted. His emotional responses, emotional management, and emotional development will likely be seriously, and perhaps permanently, impaired. The emotional processes which worked for him as a child may begin to work against him as an adult.

Who validates you in your life and makes you feel good about yourself? Who invalidates you? Violates your personal boundaries? Do you know the difference? Can you recognize it?

Allowing others to violate your personal rights is an open statement of the low level of value you assign to your personal worth. The key is to eliminate the faulty thinking that causes us to give up our power to abusers and allows them to dishonor us. Learning to manage personal boundaries is critical to healing, yet it is one of the hardest things to do because it is based on a personal understanding of our self-worth that can be pretty close to nonexistent in abuse victims.

Do you feel guilty when you say no? Victims of abuse who have low self-esteem and high codependency tendencies frequently do. If you are one of them, you are really saying no to yourself and not honoring or respecting yourself, your rights, or your authority—and you are letting others do the same. You continue to starve yourself of the emotional sustenance you need to ensure emotional health.

Managing personal boundaries, while not a cure-all, is an important place to start in emotional healing and recovery. It is also an area of your life in which applying newly learned basic skills like assertiveness and self-care can help you take your power back and accelerate your healing. Learning to be assertive—including learning how to say no when you mean it—is instrumental in protecting your personal honor, rights, and authority. It will help you regain your self-esteem and release your shame.

Appendix 1 includes a list of personal rights and authorities, along with tips on assertiveness. You can download, post, and read these to challenge your beliefs and remind you of your real value, power, and divinity. The appendix also includes tips for self-care and links to self-esteem resources, including tests and tools that you can use to gauge and improve your self-esteem.

## Setting and Achieving Goals

A goal is a planned target, destination, or achievement. A goal is intentionally set and requires a path to reach it. Setting and achieving goals are key skills to learn and develop in your healing, and this ability is a primary characteristic of people with high self-esteem.

The brain is a natural goal-setting machine. Dreams and aspirations become reality when you set goals. Achieving goals is a personal validation of our self-worth. Reaching our goals makes us happy—it's that simple.

One thing is for certain when setting goals: we need to know where we're going in order to get there. If you're traveling by car or recreational vehicle on a road trip, you can choose a destination, get a map or GPS, plan a route (or get someone to plan it for you), choose the time of year, and go. But what do you do in your life? What is your destination, map, motivation, and route? Who do you call if you get lost? The answers to these questions are complex, since we all are diverse individuals. We grow, learn, and change in different ways and at a different pace. Our experiences and perceptions are also different. What works for one person may not work for another because our strengths, weaknesses, beliefs, opportunities, and obstacles differ.

As discussed in Healing Lesson 4 in chapter 2, the thinking of victims of abuse becomes pain-avoiding rather than joy-seeking. Their deep-seated shame and low self-esteem do not nurture their drive to set and seek goals. Rather than rely on their confidence in their own abilities and accomplishments to define their self-worth, they rely on others who do not have their best interests at heart. These others may even inflict pain or manipulate them to define their worth. The solution continues to be the problem.

The challenge of setting goals and achieving them is obvious, but the consequences of not achieving them are greater. However, simply setting a goal is not a guarantee that you will achieve it.

Here are some tips to help you set and achieve goals that are also included in the healing tool kit in Appendix 1.

*Tip 1: Develop Your Personal Action and Accountability Plan*

This plan is your road map to achieving goals, getting where you want to go, and getting back on course when you get lost. Remember that your character, people skills, personal limitations, emotional makeup, and motivation level will impact achievement of goals. Mentors and coaches can help you generate your action plan, monitor your progress, hold you accountable, and develop an alternate course of actions when you hit roadblocks. The value of a coach is obvious to anyone who has watched his or her home team come back to win a title after a dismal losing streak. To develop your road map, take the following steps:

1. Write your goals down and set realistic target dates for completing them, taking into account your other commitments in life. Set goals to be the best you can be in all aspects of your life, including finances, family, spirituality, physical and emotional health, relationships, careers, social life, and community. Be sure to include short-term goals (three to six months) as well as long-term goals so you will quickly have a feeling of success. Short-term goals might include taking a class, researching a new business, or finding an exercise buddy or coach who will keep you motivated and accountable.
2. Add a target date for completing each goal.
3. Evaluate how close you are right now to achieving your short- and long-term goals. Have you achieved 10 percent of your goal or possibly even 90 percent? Identify what you need to do to fill the gap to get you to 100 percent. Remember how success will feel or sound to you when

you reach 100 percent. How will you or your loved ones benefit from achieving your goals?
4. Under or next to each goal, make a chronological list of the actions you need to take to achieve the goal. Include a target date next to each action.
5. Monitor your progress. Record and date the status next to each action. Evaluate what actions you started, which you completed, and what is stopping you from completing the others. Add sub-actions where needed to get you back on track.
6. Try not to change any due dates unless absolutely necessary. Continually changing dates can give you a false sense of security that you are on target, effective, and accountable when in fact you are not.
7. Periodically assess all aspects of your life and set new goals as needed.

*Tip 2: Make Sure Your Goals Work for You*

Change is never comfortable. In life, whatever we want to achieve has to have clear benefits. Otherwise, the challenges we face will seem impossible to overcome and not worth the effort. What are the short- and long-term benefits of achieving your goals? Identifying these benefits is essential to staying committed to achieving your goals. Success must feel good; otherwise, you will not be motivated to change.

The benefits will be different for each of us because we process information and experiences differently. Success will feel, sound, smell, and look differently to everyone. How will success look to you? How will you know you are getting closer to achieving your short-term and long-term goals?

## Tip 3: Identify Your Challenges

You are sure to face challenges and obstacles along the way that can stop you dead in your tracks. Have you identified these? What are they, and how will you deal with them or at least minimize their impact? What will you have to give up or change to achieve your goals? Are you, for example, good at delaying gratification? Do you have the self-discipline needed to succeed? If not, how will you stay on track? Perhaps you have a good friend or can hire a life coach to keep you honest. There may be people who should not know about your goals. Do you have people like this in your life?

## Tip 4: Set Realistic Goals

Goals must be attainable to be achievable. For example, I will never become a high jumper because I do not have the build, desire, or genetics to be one. We must be aware of our personal limitations when we are setting our goals so as to avoid setting ourselves up for failure.

On the other hand, we must overcome invisible psychological barriers that prevent us from setting and attaining goals. Mentors and coaches can help you identify and distinguish the differences between your limits and your limitations that can prevent you from achieving happiness in your life.

## Tip 5: Resist the Urge to Consider Accountability to Your Healing Goals as Shame

Learn to replace your triggered shame with a healthier dose of guilt, which empowers you to take responsibility and course-correct and seek help to achieve your milestones, intermediate targets, and final goals. As Michael A. Wright, PhD, advises in "Accountability Is Not Shame, but Guilt Can Be Motivating":

When you feel you have fallen short, determine whether you are responding to guilt or shame. If you are responding to guilt you will ask, "What choices did I make that were not in line with my goals? What choices can I make now to move sustainably toward my goals?" If you are responding to shame and engaging in conflict you will exclaim, "There are many reasons why I am not achieving my goals! Few people understand my struggle."

# Chapter 6

# You Have Taken Your Power Back and You Are Thriving

You cannot tap into your strength if you believe you have no power. But you've changed all that. Be proud and bask in your newfound truth. You have taken your power back. Through self-discovery and self-recovery, you have removed the emotional barriers that resulted from your traumatic beginnings that denied you access to all you are capable of being. Think back on all you've done:

- You put in the painful hard work and accountability necessary to reach your goals, regain your inner strength, build your self-esteem, create sustainable improvements in your life, and gain self-respect.
- You reversed and reengineered the original faulty design of yourself, inserted new effective self-monitoring filters, and came out a new and improved you—the authentic version you were put on this earth to be.
- You aligned your truth-based beliefs, thoughts, emotions, and actions. You are now confident that whatever life brings you, your authenticity, strength, and truth will carry you through it.
- You learned to access and rely on your own strength, and you now defend and protect your personal integrity and emotional well-being.
- You learned self-care—including self-soothing and self-coping skills—to alleviate your discomfort, build and sustain your physical and emotional health, and boost your self-esteem, self-respect, and power.

- You began to monitor and manage personal boundaries to honor and protect your self-worth.
- You found that your fears are powerless without your acknowledgment.
- You identified sources, triggers, and early warning signs of your pain and can now address them before they escalate.
- You released the shame your abusers projected onto you by accepting without judgment your powerlessness over your abusers' actions.
- You redirected your anger from yourself to the abusers who attacked you and betrayed your trust.
- You practiced self-tolerance and self-forgiveness.
- You released your distorted perceptions of your responsibility in the abuse and your associated trauma, shame, and grief—the real sources of your chronic pain.
- You replaced the pain and avoidance of your emotions with self-acceptance and self-compassion plus a newfound autonomy that will keep you accountable to your healing goals and fuel your new life.
- You started enjoying your life based on what serves you because you know you enjoy these things, know you can achieve them, and know you are worthy of them.
- You set and achieved goals in your job, health, career, finances, relationships, and spirit that bring you joy, pride, respect, self-fulfillment, and the higher-quality life you deserve.
- You resolved to pursue intimate relationships infused with respect, trust, intimacy, and mutual self-reliance.
- You freely communicated your needs, allowing healthy mutual dependency and resolving conflicts free of the concern, pain, shame, fears, and self-doubt of the past.
- You became an active complicit participant in your joy, not your abuse and exploitation.

- You used your compassion for yourself and others to give care responsibly.
- You looked into yourself with confidence for validation of your worth.
- You readily identified hurtful situations and exploitive people before they caused harm to you.
- You gauged situations accurately and shared your feelings assertively, as appropriate, without losing control of them.
- You discovered what it's like to feel emotionally strong and wake invigorated every day because you know what makes you happy, go after it, and believe you deserve it.
- You avoided exploitative job situations and could identify and pursue appropriate promotional opportunities.
- You developed your career in a way that fosters your interests and talents and accepted the financial and emotional rewards, knowing you could and would make the changes necessary to keep yourself vital and interested in your work.
- You took time out for hobbies, sports, creative arts, traveling, music, and other activities you enjoy to rejuvenate and recharge your emotional batteries.

If you have children, your new sense of self has brought you a new identity as a loving, caring parent. Your children are happy and healthy and have healed through you. You provide them with an excellent role model of emotional health and reciprocal unconditional love. You accept your children as people and raise them to respect and honor themselves and others. You foster their self-esteem by giving them appropriate amounts of power and control, and you protect them from harm by setting clear and consistent limits. You are able to discipline them using the positive elements of your relationship to hold them accountable when they fall short of the values you have set for your family. You can continue to grow together, allowing your relationship to mature ultimately into a seasoned, adult-to-adult friendship that provides joy and affiliation for the rest of your life.

This is a time to acknowledge that your family's intergenerational chain of abuse has ended with you. Take pride in your strength, courage, and abilities. Not only have you healed and taken your power back, so have your children who have healed through you. There is no greater or nobler display of love—not only to your children and loved ones but more importantly to yourself. There is no greater display of power than love for yourself and others, founded in personal truth and integrity. Your life is a living testament to this formidable accomplishment.

# Appendix 1

# Self-Help Healing Tools

This appendix contains nine recovery tools referenced throughout the book to support you through all stages of your self-discovery. You can refer to these at any time to reinforce your healing and the lessons you learned, and to refresh your skills. Also see appendix 2, "Healing Inspirational Messages."

Included in this appendix are the following nine healing tools:

1. My Personal Commitment to the Healing and Life I Deserve
2. A Look into the Future of Your Healing Journey
3. ASCA Crisis Hot-Spots Checklist
4. Tips for Dealing with Trauma, Shame, and Grief
5. Tips and Exercises for Building Self-Esteem
6. My Bill of Personal Rights
7. My Bill of Personal Authority
8. Tips for Building Assertiveness
9. Tips to Help You Set and Achieve Goals

**Healing Tool 1:**
**My Personal Commitment to the Healing and Life I Deserve**

I _____ make the following commitment to myself:

- to spend so much time improving myself and my life that I have no time for worry, judgment, criticism, whining, and complaining

- to forgive, release, and let go of my shame and my attachment to any past struggles, pain, grief, and trauma, and to allow every challenge life sends my way to make me the authentic version, the best version, of myself I was put on this earth to be
- to release my need and attachment to others to define my self-worth
- to let go of what's behind me and start appreciating the now with no worry about the past or fear for the future
- to let go of all the pointless drama, all the toxic relationships, all thoughts and behaviors that are present in my life
- to constantly shift my focus on what brings me joy and all that I am worthy of
- to make room in my heart for the love, happiness, peace, and tranquility I deserve
- to create my life from a place of infinite choices and possibilities and no longer from a place of false negative beliefs and other peoples' lies
- to honor and staying true to myself at all times and to never betray myself to please other people
- to give up on toxic thoughts, behaviors, and relationships but never on myself and my dreams, my joy, and my goals

Starting now and starting today, I will begin rebuilding my life and making it ridiculously amazing. I will honor my divinity … and honor myself always.

Sincerely,

## Healing Tool 2:
## A Look into the Future of Your Healing Journey

Here is your personal vision statement—a look into your future, not only how it will feel to recover but also to thrive.

You are no longer a victim or a survivor; you are now a victor and feel like one.

You have progressed to becoming a thriver, someone who finds joy and satisfaction in many aspects of life.

You are confident in your abilities and focus on pursuing goals that serve you and bring you pride and self-respect.

You show on the outside how you feel on the inside. You feel deserving of success and a high quality of life and are confident in your personal power.

You recognize yourself as the most important and interesting person in the world—a unique and precious part of life—and that there will never be another you in the history of creation.

You take the time and effort to nurture yourself and care for your own needs.

You have created a new family or support system for yourself that banishes the isolation and shame you felt in the past.

You can readily give of yourself to others, and you accept nurturance and consideration in return.

This is the step in which your new self comes together into a personality that expresses your full essence in the world. It feels awesome, and you embrace your new life and truth with gratitude, feeling loved and appreciated.

Intimate relationships are now infused with trust, sexual sharing, and mutual self-reliance. You freely communicate your needs, allow healthy mutual dependency, and resolve conflicts—free of the concerns, pain, shame, fears, and self-doubt of the past.

Your new self-acceptance allows you to be less critical of yourself and others, while your new self-awareness helps you to use your compassion for yourself and others responsibly. You can readily identify hurtful situations and exploitive people *before* they cause harm to you. You can gauge situations accurately and share your feelings assertively, as appropriate, without losing control of them.

You give care responsibly and look into yourself with confidence for validation of your worth. You feel emotionally strong and awake invigorated every day because you know what makes you happy and know you deserve it.

By now, you are able to avoid exploitative job situations and can identify and pursue appropriate opportunities for promotion. You are no longer mired in office politics or oppressed by bosses or authority figures because you no longer release your power or compassion to them or take on their brokenness.

You can develop your career in a way that fosters your interests and talents and accept the financial and emotional rewards that follow. If you find yourself facing a dead end in your career, you know as truth that you can make the necessary changes to keep yourself vital and interested in your work. Instead of experiencing your work and life as a strain, you now feel challenged and satisfied by both.

If you have children, your new sense of self has brought you a new identity as a loving, caring parent. Your children are happy and healthy and have healed through you. You provide them with an excellent role model of emotional health and reciprocal, unconditional love. You accept your children as people and raise them to respect and honor themselves and others. You foster their self-esteem by giving them appropriate amounts of power and control, and you protect them from harm by setting clear and consistent limits. You are able to discipline them by using the positive elements of your relationship to hold them accountable when they fall short of the values you have set for your family.

This is the time to acknowledge that your family's intergenerational chain of abuse has ended with you. You and your children are living testimony to this formidable accomplishment.

You can continue to grow together, allowing your relationship to mature into a seasoned, adult-to-adult friendship that provides joy and affiliation for the rest of your lives.

Finally, your new self begins to express itself in one area that may have always been difficult: play. You probably have neglected this area of expression, but the newly confident you may now be ready to explore this exciting domain. Hobbies, sports, creative arts, traveling, and music are just some of the many ways you can play as an adult. Playing keeps you in touch with your own inner child and affords you an opportunity to share another experience with your children. Playing revives us and recharges our emotional batteries. It improves our outlook on life and rewards us for our hard work. Don't deprive yourself of this important element of life. Find new ways of playing that fill you up and charge your active participation in life.

Many survivors wonder how they will know that they have completed their recovery. That moment is very personal, and it may or may not be related to an external event in your life. It occurs at the moment when healing on the inside and change on the outside merge into a unified sense of self. It occurs when you become your authentic self—when your beliefs, thoughts, and actions align, and you are confident that whatever life brings you, your authenticity and truth will carry you through it.

You are clear on your self-worth and personal rights and authority, and you use them routinely to pursue and achieve your goals. You balance self-care and self-compassion with giving care and compassion to others.

This moment may be a "mystical experience," one in which you feel at one with the world. It may be the moment in which you realize you have attained an achievement that symbolizes success to you. It will be different things to different people, and you are the best judge of the moment for yourself. Whichever the case, it will be beautiful. May your spiritual source guide and protect you in your search for truth.

## Healing Tool 3:
## ASCA Crisis Hot-Spots Checklist

Recovery really is possible, but it is unlikely to occur until the various crises raging in your life have been settled. Trying to initiate and proceed with recovery when your daily life is not very stable can set you up for failure. Does this apply to you? If it does, a key component will be to identify and stabilize the problem areas in your life before embarking on your recovery.

The following hot-spots checklist will help you identify and rank the issues that may be diverting energy from your recovery efforts. You may access the checklist directly at http://www.ascasupport.org/_html_manuals/survivortothriver/029_crisisHotspotChecklist.html.

Your long-term goal is to stabilize as many of your problem areas as you can. It is not necessary to fully resolve these problems—that will come as you work through recovery—but successful recovery depends on your taking steps to bring some order to your life. In so doing, you will reduce the frequency of crises and increase the amount of time and energy you can devote to your recovery.

| | Problem area? | | If yes, rate significance from 1 (lowest) to 10 (highest) |
|---|---|---|---|
| 1. Personal relationships | ○ Yes | ○ No | |
| 2. Finances | ○ Yes | ○ No | |
| 3. Parenting | ○ Yes | ○ No | |
| 4. Job | ○ Yes | ○ No | |
| 5. Housing | ○ Yes | ○ No | |
| 6. Psychological or emotional state | ○ Yes | ○ No | |

| 7. Family relationships | ○ Yes | ○ No | |
|---|---|---|---|
| 8. Addictions | ○ Yes | ○ No | |
| 9. Health issues | ○ Yes | ○ No | |
| 10. Legal issues | ○ Yes | ○ No | |

*Instructions:* Check "yes" or "no" for each area of your life and then rate the level of the problem on a scale from 1 (not a problem) to 10 (very much a problem) for any *yes* answers.

*Scoring:* Count the number of *yes* answers and then rank them from highest (most problematic) to lowest (least problematic) score.

*Goal:* Start with the three highest-ranking problems on the checklist, or choose those that cause the greatest instability in your life.

*Action plan:* Document the top three most significant areas below on the hot-spots list. Focus on each of these three key problem areas and try to determine how you might stabilize each over the long term. If you need help, contact a trusted friend, therapist, or coach.

It may take some time and thought to come up with truly valuable ideas, but unless you start this process, you are likely to delay your recovery and continue to operate in crisis mode.

**Hot spot #1:** _____
Things I can try: _____

**Hot spot #2:** _____
Things I can try: _____

_____
_____
_____
_____
_____
_____

**Hot spot #3:** _____
Things I can try: _____

_____
_____
_____
_____
_____
_____

**Healing Tool 4:**
**Tips for Dealing with Trauma, Shame, and Grief**

*Tip 1: Create a Healing Mind-Set*

- Turn your compassion and tolerance toward yourself and accept your feelings and yourself—warts and all—as a valuable person.
- Educate yourself on trauma, shame, and grief, and their debilitating effects.
- Learn to identify the feelings of emotional pain, trauma, shame, and guilt as they occur in your daily life. Write in a journal about situations and relationships that trigger

them. Learn to bring these events into your level of awareness and identify these triggers (see Tip 2 below).
- Challenge your emotions. Ask yourself which ones result from lack of compassion and tolerance for yourself. For example, "Even though I feel sad, I am still a caring person, able to go to work and take care of my children."
- Work on these areas as traumatic-pain trigger points and do what you can to avoid them or minimize their harmful effects.
- Get rid of toxic friends who habitually violate your trust and your personal boundaries.
- Be consistent and fair about sharing your compassion and tolerance with yourself as well as with others.
- Go first with your compassion. Learn to be tolerant of yourself first. Know when to quit, rest, and say you have had enough. This is not selfish. This is self-preservation and what emotionally healthy people do.
- Respect your own personal boundaries. Demonstrate kindness and acceptance to honor yourself. Do not violate your own personal wishes, body, trust, time, privacy, feelings, and property.
- Do not let other people violate your personal boundaries. See chapter 5 on "Building Self-Esteem and Self-Compassion."
- Stop defending your feelings, preferences, trust, time, and choices to abusers. Abusers use this as an opportunity to abuse you more and expose you to more trauma and shame. If you must respond to their sneaky insults or criticism, just say, "That's interesting. Let me think about it." Then ignore them and turn their comments into a non-issue.
- Focus on gratitude for what you have. My mother told me if you have food, a roof over your head, your health, and people who love you, you have everything. She was right.

- Avoid black-and-white thinking that focuses only on good or bad outcomes.
- Refrain from complaining about what you disagree with or do not like in yourself. If you have nothing nice to say or think about yourself, don't say or think it. Look at your track record for evidence of success and to learn acceptance and tolerance.
- Welcome and view disagreements from trusted individuals or differences not as criticism but as motivation to learn more and become a person of integrity.
- Give yourself a break. Be careful to understand the difference between rejecting the sin and rejecting the sinner. Learn to say "who cares?" more.
- Don't judge a book by its cover. Don't rush to judgment. Refrain from developing an opinion before you get all the facts. If in doubt, ask a wise and trusted friend.
- Refrain from making yourself the brunt of jokes or laughter.
- Do not always stand in the back of the line. Allow yourself to go first sometimes.

*Tip 2: Learn Your Triggers and Early Warning Signs and Address Them before They Escalate*

- Implementing constructive solutions is where confidence and mastery come from. If you find yourself triggered into stress, anxiety, self-loathing, sadness, grief, or trauma, ask yourself "Is this a problem that I need to deal with on my own, or with the help of others or both? Does it require change or acceptance?"
- Acknowledge your painful feelings. This can be a challenge if you've been criticized or unsupported when experiencing difficult emotions in the past. Understanding the causes of challenging emotions helps you predict and

possibly avoid these situations. From there you can make choices about how to deal with reoccurring patterns of negative thinking or interpersonal situations that can cause problems.
- Express your emotions by writing them down. It is also important to write down what happened to make you feel upset, and how you plan to deal with it.
- Identify personal strengths that can help you at this time. After all, you've survived so far and taken care of yourself, so you have a track record of landing on your feet. Let this help you develop a realistic, optimistic, caring attitude toward yourself.
- If you identify any weak areas within yourself that need strengthening, make a plan to develop more resilience. For example, if you lack confidence, you need a strategy to foster more faith in yourself. Do you need to build more personal stamina, or is it more a question of softening your attitude toward yourself?
- It may be helpful to talk about your pain and your strengths with a nonjudgmental friend, support group, or counselor who can see the abilities that you minimize and don't see in yourself.

*Tip 3: Resist the Urge to Consider Accountability to Your Healing Goals as Shame*

In "Accountability Is Not Shame, but Guilt Can Be Motivating," Michael A. Wright, PhD, gives this advice:

> When you feel you have fallen short, determine whether you are responding to guilt or shame. If you are responding to guilt you will ask, "What choices did I make that were not in line with my goals? What choices can I make now to

move sustainably toward my goals?" If you are responding to shame and engaging in conflict you will exclaim, "There are many reasons why I am not achieving my goals! Few people understand my struggle."

Learn to replace your triggered shame with a healthier dose of guilt, which empowers you to take responsibility and seek help to achieve your recovery goals.

*Tip 4: Take Anger Management Classes*

Shame triggers anger, which can lead to interpersonal conflicts in addition to unnecessary angst. Anger management classes can help you compassionately identify the sources of your fears and frustrations, validate these feelings, and provide constructive coping and communication strategies to manage them before they escalate.

*Tip 5: Look at Your Track Record from Youth*

Recall people in your childhood who had something good to say about you—those who were kind to you, like teachers, clergy, neighbors, a surrogate parent, or perhaps a relative. What words did they use to describe your best qualities? How did you feel when you were around them? Revive these important people from your past by writing about them in a journal and exploring what their support meant to you, then and now.

*Tip 6: Look to a Higher Power*

If you are religious or spiritual, turn to your Higher Power or Source to cleanse you of the shame and unworthiness you feel so deeply. Religion and spiritual practice can be tremendous sources of inner sustenance and provide an ideal vision to replace the negative role models and scenarios of the past.

## Tip 7: Get Good Feedback

Good feedback is honest, constructive, and unbiased. Share your struggles with working this step on support blogs, group therapy meetings, a wise and trusted friend, and Facebook self-help communities like Yourlifelifter and After Narcissistic Abuse.

## Tip 8: Learn the Signs of Trauma-Bonding

As discussed in Healing Lesson 6 in chapter 2, if you have any of the symptoms of trauma-bonding, your trauma must be treated like an addiction. You are not thinking of your abuser because of love and some sort of soul-connected mystical control he or she has over you. The abuser is your drug, and the severity of the abuse has caused chemical changes in your brain that have created a trauma addiction. Please seek out professional therapy.

When we recover from addictions, we will have cravings during times of stress. This is why we think of our abusers. You're not missing that individual in the sense that you miss an abusive and dangerous predator; you miss the addiction to the cycles that individual created. The craving is what causes a relapse.

The idea is to get enough time away from the trauma source to heal our brains. This is why no contact with your abuser is warranted for our healing. You must also change situations in your life that trigger cravings. Use support systems from therapy and support groups, and change any daily habits you had with the abuser.

You need to change your thinking patterns, be very good to yourself, be kind and compassionate, and learn skills that will keep you feeling safe in the present moment. This includes traditional and alternative therapies, such as meditation, prayer, yoga, exercise, or whatever will move your thought processes away from the abuser and toward your own self-care and self-soothing. See Tips 9, 10, and 11 below.

*Tip 9: Regain Control through Rhythmical Movement*

Take classes in rhythmical movement like yoga and tango dancing to get back in charge of your body. Renowned trauma expert Dr. Bessel van der Kolk has pioneered the use of yoga as a therapy that is helping individuals work through their PTSD. He reports in *The Body Keeps the Score: Brain, Mind, and Body in the Healing of Trauma* that the issue of self-regulation needs to be front and center in the treatment of traumatized people.

Yoga teaches those who feel trapped in their memory sensations that emotions can come to an end. It allows those suffering from traumatic stress to observe that discomfort can be tolerated until they shift into a different posture when the emotions end. Rhythmical movements help us reintegrate the personal rhythms that we lose when we are traumatized. Both teach us that there are things we can do—other than take legal or illegal medications—to quiet the brain and reintegrate not only with ourselves but also with others from whom trauma has separated us.

*Tip 10: Consider Other Alternative Therapies*

Proven effective therapies for releasing pain and trauma include hypnotherapy, Eye Movement Desensitization and Reprocessing (EMDR), Emotional Freedom Techniques based on acupressure, and the Quanta Freedom Healing system by narcissistic abuse recovery expert Melanie Tonia Evans.

*Tip 11: Seek Professional Therapy*

The ASCA recommends finding a professional therapist if you are not progressing in your healing and recovery. You may be trauma-addicted or suffering from toxic traumatic stress and chronic shame and grief.

In order to resolve pain addictions, an ongoing reparative relationship with a qualified therapist can help you challenge your internal self-critical dialogue and replace it with a healthier one. A therapist can also help you find words to communicate your internal feelings of powerlessness and fear, validate them, and free you from being locked inside yourself.

If you experience exaggerated shame, a competent therapist is an important ally in helping you transform the shame into self-acceptance. Talk about your shame with your therapist and share how you experienced shame in your childhood and in your life, including in your therapy sessions. With your therapist's help, identify the ways in which you keep yourself from feeling your shame by adopting a role or false self that you portray for others based on what you think is acceptable to them rather than yourself.

Share this false self with your therapist and try to understand what the role gives you that you feel you lack. This can help you hone in on shame triggers you can work to acknowledge, challenge, release, and replace with new rational beliefs and emotions that support your emotional health and well-being.

**Healing Tool 5:**
**Tips and Exercises for Building Self-Esteem\***

*\*Adapted (except where noted) from "Building Self-Esteem: A Self-Help Guide" from the U.S. Department of Health and Human Services (DHHS), Substance Abuse and Mental Health Services*

*Administration (SAMHSA), and Center for Mental Health Services (CMHS).*

People with a healthy level of self-esteem share the following characteristics:

- They firmly believe in certain values and principles, and they are ready to defend those values and principles even when finding opposition, feeling secure enough to modify them in light of experience.
- They are able to act according to what they consider to be the best choice, trusting their own judgment and not feeling guilty when others do not agree.
- They do not lose time worrying excessively about what happened in the past nor about what could happen in the future. They learn from the past and plan for the future, but they live in the present intensely.
- They fully trust in their capacity to solve problems, not hesitating after failures and difficulties. They ask others for help when they need it.
- They consider themselves equal in dignity to others, rather than inferior or superior, while accepting differences in certain talents, personal prestige, or financial standing.
- They understand the ways in which they are interesting and valuable person to others, at least for those with whom they have a friendship.
- They resist manipulation and collaborate with others only if it seems appropriate and convenient.
- They admit and accept different internal feelings and drives, either positive or negative, revealing those drives to others only when they choose.
- They are able to enjoy a great variety of activities.

- They are sensitive to the feelings and needs of others, respect generally accepted social rules, and claim no right or desire to prosper at another's expense.
- They use their compassion responsibly to their own and others' benefit.
- They understand well what their personal boundaries and authority are and understand their right to have theirs respected.
- They can work toward finding solutions and voice discontent without belittling themselves or others when challenges arise.

How many of these describe you? Which ones do you feel you need to work on? Answering these questions can help you gauge where you are in recovery and where you need to focus and set some milestones and goals. Use the tips and exercises that follow to work on improving your self-esteem.

*Things You Can Do Right Away to Raise Your Self-Esteem*

As you were growing up, you may not have learned how to take good care of yourself. In fact, much of your attention may have been on taking care of others, on just getting by, or on behaving according to someone else's standards. Begin today to take good care of yourself. Treat yourself as a wonderful parent would treat a small child or as one very best friend might treat another. If you work at taking good care of yourself, you will find that you feel better about yourself. Here are some suggestions:

- *Pay attention to your own needs and wants.* Listen to what your body, your mind, and your heart are telling you. For instance, if your body is telling you that you have been sitting down too long, stand up and stretch. If your heart is longing to spend more time with a special friend, do

it. If your mind is telling you to clean up your basement, listen to your favorite music, or stop thinking bad thoughts about yourself, take those ideas seriously.
- *Eat healthy foods and avoid junk foods* (foods containing a lot of sugar, salt, or fat). A healthy daily diet is usually five or six servings of vegetables and fruit; six servings of whole-grain foods like bread, pasta, cereal, and rice; and two servings of protein foods like beef, chicken, fish, cheese, cottage cheese, or yogurt.
- *Exercise.* Moving your body helps you to feel better and improves your self-esteem. Arrange a time every day or as often as possible when you can get some exercise, preferably outdoors. You can do many different things. Taking a walk is the most common. You could run, ride a bicycle, play a sport, climb up and down stairs several times, put on a tape, or play the radio and dance to the music—anything that feels good to you. If you have a health problem that restricts your ability to exercise, check with your doctor before beginning or changing your exercise habits.
- *Do special personal hygiene tasks* to pamper and make you feel better about yourself, such as a bubble bath, special hair conditioning or styling, manicures and pedicures, and teeth whitening.
- *Have a physical examination* every year to make sure you are in good health.
- *Plan fun activities for yourself.* Learn new things every day.
- *Take time to do things you enjoy.* You may be so busy, or feel so badly about yourself, that you spend little or no time doing things you enjoy, such as playing a musical instrument, doing a craft project, flying a kite, or going fishing. Make a list of things you enjoy doing. Then do something from that list every day. Add to the list anything new that you discover you enjoy doing.

- *Get something done that you have been putting off.* Clean out that drawer. Wash that window. Write that letter. Pay that bill.
- *Do things that make use of your own special talents and abilities.* For instance, if you are good with your hands, make things for yourself, family, and friends. If you like animals, consider having a pet or at least playing with friends' pets.
- *Dress in clothes that make you feel good about yourself.* If you have little money to spend on new clothes, check out thrift stores in your area.
- *Give yourself rewards for being a great person*, such as listening to your favorite music, reading your favorite books, or taking a trip to a museum.
- *Spend time with people who treat you well* and make you feel good about yourself. Avoid people who treat you badly.
- *Make your living space a place that honors the person you are.* Whether you live in a single room, a small apartment, or a large home, make that space comfortable and attractive for you. If you share your living space with others, have some space that is just for you, a place where you can keep your things and know that they will not be disturbed and that you can decorate any way you choose.
- *Display items that you find attractive* or that remind you of your achievements or of special times or people in your life. If cost is a factor, use your creativity to think of inexpensive or free ways that you can add to the comfort and enjoyment of your space.
- *Make mealtime special.* Turn off the television, radio, and stereo. Set the table, even if you are eating alone. Light a candle or put some flowers or an attractive object in the center of the table. Arrange your food in an attractive way on your plate. If you eat with others, encourage discussion

of pleasant topics. Avoid discussing difficult issues at meals.
- *Take advantage of opportunities to learn something new* or improve your skills. Take a class or go to a seminar. Many adult-education programs are free or very inexpensive. For those that are more costly, ask about a possible scholarship or fee reduction.
- *Begin doing things that you know will make you feel better about yourself,* like going on a diet, beginning an exercise program, or keeping your living space clean.
- *Do something nice for another person.* Smile at someone who looks sad. Say a few kind words to the checkout cashier. Help your spouse with an unpleasant chore. Take a meal to a friend who is sick. Send a card to an acquaintance. Volunteer for a worthy organization.
- *Make it a point to treat yourself well every day.* Before you go to bed each night, write about how you treated yourself well during the day.

You may be doing some of these things already. There will be others you need to work on. You will find that you will continue to learn new and better ways to take care of yourself. As you incorporate these changes into your life, your self-esteem will continue to improve.

*Changing Negative Thoughts about Yourself to Positive Ones*

You may be giving yourself negative messages about yourself. Many people do. These are messages that you learned when you were young. You learned from many different sources, including other children, your teachers, family members, caregivers, even the media and the general prejudice and stigma in our society.

Once you learned these negative messages, you may have repeated them over and over to yourself, especially when you were not feeling well or when you were having a hard time. You may have come to believe them. You may have even worsened the problem by making up some negative messages or thoughts of your own. These negative thoughts or messages make you feel bad about yourself and lower your self-esteem.

Some examples of common negative messages that people repeat over and over to themselves include "I am a jerk," "I am a loser," "I never do anything right," "No one would ever like me," "I am a klutz." Most people believe such messages, no matter how untrue or unreal. The messages come to mind immediately in the right circumstance. For instance, if you get a wrong answer, you think, "I am so stupid." The messages may include words like *should*, *ought*, or *must*. They tend to assume the worst about everything and everyone—especially you—and they are hard to turn off or unlearn.

You may think these thoughts or give yourself these negative messages so often that you are hardly aware of them. Start paying attention. Carry a small pad with you as you go about your daily routine for several days and jot down negative thoughts about yourself whenever you notice them. Some people say they notice more negative thinking when they are tired, sick, or dealing with a lot of stress. As you become aware of your negative thoughts, you may notice more and more of them.

It helps to take a closer look at your negative thought patterns to check out whether or not they are true. You may want a close friend or counselor to help you with this. When you are in a good mood and when you have a positive attitude about yourself, ask yourself the following questions about each negative thought you have noticed:

- Is this message really true?
- Would a person say this to another person? If not, why am I saying it to myself?
- What do I get out of thinking this thought? If it makes me feel badly about myself, why not stop thinking it?

You could also ask someone else who likes you and who you trust if you should believe this thought about yourself. Often, just looking at a thought or situation in a new light helps bring clarity.

The next step in this process is to develop positive statements you can say to yourself to replace these negative thoughts whenever you notice yourself thinking them. You can't think two opposing thoughts at the same time. When you are thinking a positive thought about yourself, you can't be thinking a negative one. In developing these thoughts, use positive words like *happy, peaceful, loving, enthusiastic, warm*. Use the following table as an example:

| Negative Thought | Positive Thought |
|---|---|
| I am not worth anything. | I am a valuable person. |
| I have never accomplished anything. | I have accomplished many things. |
| I always make mistakes. | I do many things well. |
| I am a jerk. | I am a great person. |
| I don't deserve a good life. | I deserve to be happy and healthy. |
| I am stupid. | I am smart. |

Avoid using negative words, such as *worried, frightened, upset, tired, bored, not, never, can't*. Don't make a statement like "I am not going to worry anymore." Instead, say "I focus on the positive" or whatever feels right to you. Substitute "it would be nice if" for "should." Always use the present tense—"I am healthy, I am well, I am happy, I have a good job"—as if the condition already exists. Use *I, me*, or your own name.

Try this exercise: Fold a piece of paper in half the long way to make two columns. In one column, write your negative thoughts, and in the other column, write a positive thought that contradicts each negative thought. Work on changing your negative thoughts to positive ones by doing the following:

- replacing the negative thought with the positive one every time you realize you are thinking the negative thought.
- repeating your positive thought over and over to yourself out loud whenever you get a chance and even sharing them with another person if possible.
- writing them over and over.
- making signs that say the positive thought, hanging them in places where you would see them often (like on your refrigerator door or on the mirror in your bathroom), and repeating the thought to yourself several times when you see it.

It helps to reinforce the positive thought if you repeat it over and over to yourself when you are deeply relaxed, like when you are doing a deep-breathing or relaxation exercise, or when you are just falling asleep or waking up.

Changing the negative thoughts you have about yourself to positive ones takes time and persistence. If you use these and the following techniques consistently for four to six weeks, you will notice that you don't think negative thoughts about yourself as much. If they recur at some other time, you can repeat these activities. Don't give up. You deserve to think good thoughts about yourself.

*Exercises to Help You Feel Good about Yourself*

Any of the following activities will help you feel better about yourself and reinforce your self-esteem over the long term. Read through them and do those that seem most comfortable to you. You may want to defer some of the other activities to another time, while others you may want to repeat again and again. Pick the ones that best suit you and fulfill your needs.

**Exercise 1:**
**Challenge Your Inner Critic**

Psychotherapist Pete Walker, in "Shrinking the Inner Critic in Complex PTSD," explains that our fruitless childhood efforts to be accepted and validated by abusive and neglectful parents can make us hypervigilant and desperate to relieve our fears, anxieties, and emotional pain, including shame. We can come to believe that even our basic needs are imperfections. We become hypercritical as well. Recovering individuals must learn to challenge and disconnect from the many inner-critic processes that bring them back to their feelings of overwhelming fear, self-hate, and hopelessness rooted in childhood. Our inner critic, he explains, weds shame and self-hate about imperfection to adult fear of abandonment and false beliefs of powerlessness and need for perfectionism.

Here is Pete Walker's list of fourteen common inner criticisms, paired with very effective healthier thought-substitution responses you can use to challenge, tame, and diffuse your inner critic's negative and abusive self-talk.

1. *Perfectionism*
   Perfectionism can arise as an attempt to gain safety and support in my dangerous family. Perfection is a self-persecutory myth. I do not have to be perfect to be safe or loved in the present. I am letting go of relationships that require perfection. I have a right to make mistakes.

Mistakes do not make me a mistake. Every mistake or mishap is an opportunity to practice loving myself in the places I have never been loved.

2. *All-or-None and Black-and-White Thinking*
I reject extreme or overgeneralized descriptions, judgments, or criticisms. One negative happenstance does not mean I am stuck in a never-ending pattern of defeat. Statements that describe me as "always" or "never" this or that, are typically grossly inaccurate.

3. *Self-Hate, Self-Disgust, and Toxic Shame*
I commit to myself. I am on my side. I am a good enough person. I refuse to trash myself. I turn shame back into blame and disgust, and externalize it to anyone who shames my normal feelings and foibles. As long as I am not hurting anyone, I refuse to be shamed for normal emotional responses like anger, sadness, fear, and depression. I especially refuse to attack myself for how hard it is to completely eliminate the self-hate habit.

4. *Micromanagement/Worrying/Obsessing/Looping/Over-Futurizing*
I will not repetitively examine details over and over. I will not jump to negative conclusions. I will not endlessly second-guess myself. I cannot change the past. I forgive all my past mistakes. I cannot make the future perfectly safe. I will stop hunting for what could go wrong. I will not try to control the uncontrollable. I will not micromanage myself or others. I work in a way that is "good enough," and I accept the existential fact that my efforts sometimes bring desired results and sometimes they do not. "God grant me the serenity to accept the things I cannot change, the courage to change the things I can, and the wisdom to know the difference."—The Serenity Prayer

5. *Unfair/Devaluing Comparisons*
   To others or to one's most perfect moments. I refuse to compare myself unfavorably to others. I will not compare "my insides to their outsides." I will not judge myself for not being at peak performance all the time. In a society that pressures us into acting happy all the time, I will not get down on myself for feeling bad.
6. *Guilt*
   Feeling guilty does not mean I am guilty. I refuse to make my decisions and choices from guilt; sometimes I need to feel the guilt and do it anyway. In the inevitable instance when I inadvertently hurt someone, I will apologize, make amends, and let go of my guilt. I will not apologize over and over. I am no longer a victim. I will not accept unfair blame. Guilt is sometimes camouflaged fear. I am afraid, but I am not guilty or in danger.
7. *Shoulding*
   I will substitute the words "want to" for "should" and only follow this imperative if it feels like I want to, unless I am under legal, ethical, or moral obligation.
8. *Overproductivity/Workaholism/Busyholism*
   I am a human being not a human doing. I will not choose to be perpetually productive. I am more productive in the long run, when I balance work with play and relaxation. I will not try to perform at 100 percent all the time. I subscribe to the normalcy of vacillating along a continuum of efficiency.
9. *Harsh Judgments of Self and Others/Name-Calling*
   I will not let the bullies and critics of my early life win by joining and agreeing with them. I refuse to attack myself or abuse others. I will not displace the criticism and blame that rightfully belongs to them onto myself or current people in my life.

10. *Drasticizing/Catastrophizing/Hypochondrisizing*
    I feel afraid but I am not in danger. I am not "in trouble" with my parents. I will not blow things out of proportion. I refuse to scare myself with thoughts and pictures of my life deteriorating. No more homemade horror movies and disaster flicks.
11. *Negative Focus*
    I renounce over-noticing and dwelling on what might be wrong with me or life around me. I will not minimize or discount my attributes. Right now, I notice, visualize, and enumerate my accomplishments, talents, and qualities, as well as the many gifts that life offers me, e.g., friends, nature, music, film, food, beauty, color, pets, etc.
12. *Time Urgency*
    I am not in danger. I do not need to rush. I will not hurry unless it is a true emergency. I am learning to enjoy doing my daily activities at a relaxed pace.
13. *Performance Anxiety*
    I reduce procrastination by reminding myself that I will not accept unfair criticism or perfectionist expectations from anyone. Even when afraid, I will defend myself from unfair criticism. I won't let fear make my decisions.
14. *Perseverating about Being Attacked*
    Unless there are clear signs of danger, I will thought-stop my projection of past bullies/critics onto others. The vast majority of my fellow human beings are peaceful people. I have legal authorities to aid in my protection if threatened by the few who aren't. I invoke thoughts and images of my friends' love and support.

## Exercise 2:
## Make Affirming Lists

Making affirming lists, rereading them often, and rewriting them from time to time will help you feel better about yourself. If you have a journal, you can write your lists there. If you don't, any piece of paper will do. Make a list of the following:

- at least five of your strengths, such as persistence, courage, friendliness, creativity
- at least five things you admire about yourself, such as the way you have raised your children, your good relationship with your brother, or your spirituality
- the five greatest achievements in your life so far, such as recovering from a serious illness, graduating from high school or college, or learning to use a computer
- at least twenty accomplishments, from something as simple as learning to tie your shoes to getting an advanced college degree
- ten ways you can "treat" or reward yourself that don't include food and that don't cost anything, such as walking in woods, window-shopping, watching children playing on a playground, gazing at a baby's face or at a beautiful flower, or chatting with a friend
- ten things you can do to make yourself laugh
- ten things you could do to help someone else
- ten things that you do that make you feel good about yourself.

## Exercise 3:
## Reinforcing a Positive Self-Image

To do this exercise, you will need a piece of paper, a pencil or pen, and a timer or clock. Any kind of paper will do, but if you have paper and pen you really like, that will be even better.

Set a timer for ten minutes or note the time on your watch or a clock. Write your name across the top of the paper. Then write everything positive and good you can think of about yourself. Include special attributes, talents, and achievements.

You can use single words or sentences, whichever you prefer. You can write the same things over and over if you want to emphasize them. Don't worry about spelling or grammar. Your ideas don't have to be organized.

Write down whatever comes to mind. You are the only one who will see this paper. Avoid making any negative statements or using any negative words—only positive ones.

When the ten minutes are up, read the paper over to yourself. You may feel sad when you read it over because it is a new, different, and positive way of thinking about yourself—a way that contradicts some of the negative thoughts you may have had. Those feelings will diminish as your reread this paper.

Read the paper over again several times. Put it in a convenient place, such as your pocket, purse, wallet, or the table beside your bed. Read it over to yourself several times a day or more to keep reminding yourself of how great you are. Find a private space and read it aloud. If you can, read it to a supportive friend or family member.

## Exercise 4:
## Developing Positive Affirmations

Affirmations are positive statements about yourself that make you feel better. They describe ways you would like to feel about yourself all the time. They may not, however, describe how you feel about yourself right now. The following examples of affirmations will help you in making your own list of affirmations:

- I feel good about myself.
- I take good care of myself. I eat right, get plenty of exercise, do things I enjoy, get good health care, and attend to my personal hygiene needs.
- I spend my time with people who are nice to me and make me feel good about myself.
- I am a good person.
- I deserve to be alive.
- Many people like me.

Make a list of your own affirmations. Keep this list in a handy place, like your pocket or purse. You may want to make copies of your list so you can have them in several different places for easy access. Read the affirmations over and over to yourself aloud whenever you can. Share them with others when you feel like it. Write them down from time to time. As you do this, the affirmations tend to gradually become true for you. You gradually come to feel better and better about yourself.

**Exercise 5:
Create a Personal "Celebratory Scrapbook" to Honor Yourself**

Develop an "all about me" scrapbook that celebrates you and the wonderful person you are. Include pictures of yourself at different ages, writings you enjoy, mementos of things you have done and places you have been, cards you have received, etc. Or set up a place in your home that celebrates "you." It could be on a bureau, shelf, or table. Decorate the space with objects that remind you of the special person you are. If you don't have a private space that you can leave set up, put the objects in a special bag, box, or your purse and set them up in the space whenever you do this work. Take them out and look at them whenever you need to bolster your self-esteem.

## Exercise 6:
## Appreciation Exercise

At the top of a sheet of paper, write "I like [your name] because:" and have friends, acquaintances, and family members write an appreciative statement about you in the space below. When you read these statements, don't deny them and don't argue with what has been written, just accept it! Read this paper over and over. Keep it in a place where you will see it often.

## Exercise 7:
## Create a Self-Esteem Calendar

Get a calendar with large blank spaces for each day. Schedule into each day some small thing you would enjoy doing, similar to the following:

- go into a flower shop and smell the flowers
- call my sister
- draw a sketch of my cat
- buy a new DVD
- tell my daughter I love her
- bake brownies
- lie in the sun for twenty minutes
- wear my favorite scent

Now make a commitment to check your "enjoy life" calendar every day and do whatever you have scheduled for yourself.

## Exercise 8:
## Mutual Complimenting Exercise

Get together for ten minutes with a person you like and trust. Set a timer for five minutes or note the time on a watch or clock. One of you begins by complimenting the other person and saying everything positive about the other person for the first five minutes. Then the other person does the same thing for the next five minutes. Notice how you feel about yourself before and after this exercise. Repeat it often.

*Research Self-Esteem Resources*

Research resources on and exercises for building self-esteem and self-compassion. Try some of the suggested activities. Here are some links to information and free self-esteem and self-compassion tests and exercises:

- http://psychologytoday.tests.psychtests.com/bin/transfer?req=MTF8MzIwN3w0Njc2MTIzfD-F8MQ%3D%3D&refempt
- http://www.counseling.ufl.edu/cwc/uploads/docs/Sorensen_Self-Esteem_Test.pdf
- http://www.esteemedself.com/exercises/
- http://www.self-compassion.org
- http://core.eqi.org/eqe2012d.pdf
- http://www.pete-walker.com

## Healing Tool 6:
## My Bill of Personal Rights

Post and read this daily:
I deserve the following rights and freedoms anytime, anywhere, and with anyone:

- the right to be happy and seek joy
- the freedom to regulate my thoughts and emotions without input from another person and without defending what I feel and believe
- freedom of choice
- the freedom to say what I please and the wisdom to know when to say it
- the right to set personal boundaries on my time, feelings, expectations, money, sleep, property, and body
- the right to always have my personal boundaries respected
- the freedom to protect myself in a responsible and mature manner
- the freedom to ask for what I want and need and the wisdom to know when and whom to ask
- the right to have my needs and wants met
- the right to exercise my innate creative abilities
- the freedom to say no when dictated by my best interests
- the right to respectful and dignified treatment
- the right to know who I really am, unhindered and without others' tainted filters
- the freedom to know what I want
- the freedom to choose the life, food, clothes, friends, home, education, partner, lifestyle, religion, career, home, or whatever I want
- the right to assert my likes and dislikes
- the right to voice my opinion
- the right to accept myself for who I am
- the right to accept compliments
- the right to love and like whomever I choose
- the right to be successful and to celebrate and be recognized for my success without insults, fear, jealousy, envy, denigration, diminishment, or reprisal
- the freedom to cultivate and communicate my interests and points of view

- the freedom to tolerate points of view that differ from mine
- the right to accommodate or help another person without losing my own identity or bank account
- the right to assert my rights without fear of rejection or abandonment
- the right to assert my rights without fear of physical or mental punishment or other reprisals
- the right to be likable and lovable in a healthy manner without pain and suffering
- the right to pursue my own interests
- the right to spend money I have earned on whatever I want
- the right to be healthy and fit
- the right to abundance
- the right to make mistakes
- the right to not be perfect
- the right to pursue my goals

**Healing Tool 7:
My Bill of Personal Authority**

Post and read this daily:
I allow myself the freedom and I demand the right to exercise my authority to do the following:

- recognize myself as the most important and interesting person in the world—a unique and precious part of life—and that there will never be another me in the history of creation
- love myself
- gain the skills, knowledge, and abilities to make the best decisions I can for myself
- go after my dreams

- live a harmonious, peaceful, angst-free life
- be the best I can be for myself
- obtain personal validation from myself
- feel warm and happy, kind, and loving toward myself
- be selfish and take the time and effort to care for my own needs
- be treated with decency and respect by everyone and treat others accordingly
- realize that my character may be better than others
- realize that at my divine center I am no better or worse, or more or less important, than anyone else in the entire world
- be different, make mistakes, be wrong
- take the time and effort to fulfill my own needs
- succeed and live a quality of life I aspire to
- be financially and emotionally independent
- be open and kind, loving, and lovable—compassionate and helpful without pain and self-sacrifice
- be healthy and energetic
- feel bad sometimes and to have "unacceptable" thoughts, images, desires, and experiences
- change my mind
- be emotional—love, to cry, to be angry
- be genuine—not fulfill others' images of me
- accept constructive criticism and request input from those I trust
- ask for help and accept help when I need it
- make mistakes and learn from them
- be loyal, courageous, and exceptional in both my personal and professional life

## Healing Tool 8:
## Tips for Building Assertiveness

The right to regulate our own emotions is the foundation of all other personal rights and sets up a barrier against manipulation and pain. It also allows us to pursue happiness and joy. Learning assertiveness—including how to say no—is instrumental in not only protecting this right but all rights that support our self-esteem and prevent us from being manipulated and abused by those who push our pain and shame buttons. Assertiveness allows us to peacefully do the following:

- be concerned with our own needs, with due consideration for other people's needs
- be openly able to express ourselves with other people
- respond in a respectful manner when there is a disagreement
- be able to ask for help when we need it
- be confident and able to make decisions
- be able to say no to people, places, and situations that do not serve us
- be responsible for our own feelings, behaviors, thoughts, and self-worth without dependence on others.

Assertiveness supports thoughtful, open, and respectful communication and reassures people that you will not hinder or impede their rights or authority, even if you disagree. This leaves room for whatever compromise is possible.

*How to Develop More Assertiveness*

Replacing old feelings of defenselessness, powerlessness, and aggressiveness with assertiveness can be difficult. Breaking old habits takes practice, so be patient. It's okay to make a few mistakes along the way.

In order to respond assertively, try phrasing your response or your request using what is called a DESC script. This script was developed by Sharon and Gordon Bower and is detailed in their book *Asserting Yourself*. DESC stands for:

| | |
|---|---|
| **D**escribe | Describe the behavior/situation as completely and objectively as possible. Just the facts! "The last time my sister came to visit, I cleaned the entire house all by myself." |
| **E**xpress | Express your feelings and thoughts about the situation/behavior: "As a result, I felt exhausted and stressed out." Try to phrase your statements using *I* and not *you*. Beginning sentences with *you* often puts people on the defensive, which means they won't listen. |
| **S**pecify | Specify what behavior/outcome you would prefer: "I would like the two of us to work on cleaning the house the next time we have visitors." |
| **C**onsequences | Specify the consequences (both positive and negative): "If we both work together, the house will be cleaned up faster, and we can all enjoy the visit together." |

Try writing the script out and practicing it before you talk to the person. Pay attention to your nonverbal behavior as well. Use good eye contact and stand tall.

*How to Say No and Mean It*

Saying no comfortably is an important component of learning to be assertive. It helps you develop boundaries and can safeguard your time, energy, and personal rights. In some cases, saying no effectively may even help keep you safe from harm. "No" is a complete sentence that requires no justification. Simply saying no or "no, thank you" is all that is needed. You may need to repeat "no" again. You may not want to engage in any further conversation with manipulators or abusers where you feel pressured to concede to their wishes and give up your power to them. Try using the "broken record" method and repeat what you want in a calm, collected manner, offering no explanations or rationalizations.

*How to Respond Positively to Criticism*

People often use criticism to push your vulnerability buttons and get you to do what they want or give them what they want. Most people react to criticism with anxiety, denial, and defensiveness. If you learn how to deal with what pushes your buttons, you can protect what is valuable to you and keep your emotions in check.

Instead of reacting to criticism with denials or counterattacks that lead to more attacks, the Bowers suggest you try agreeing only to whatever is true in the statement. That forces you to listen carefully and respond to what someone says rather than defend against implied insult and the pain it triggers.

Others may criticize you when you make a mistake, but if you think about your response, you can filter out the shame and be better able to honor your personal rights and preferences. To better cope with shame, "assertively accept" the negative and ask questions to encourage the critic to respond constructively rather than manipulatively.

For example, when someone says, "You don't know how to do XYZ," you could interpret it to mean that there is something wrong with you and respond defensively with a statement like, "I can do lots of things." This may drive the critic to develop a longer list of things you can't do, escalating rather than soothing your pain triggers and causing the interaction to degrade into a very harmful one. Now replace the defensive response with what you agree to be true and challenge it with: "I don't understand. What is it about how I do XYZ that bothers you?" If you receive an answer like, "I'd prefer not to be responsible for XYZ all the time," you have found the real issue. Remember, too, that you always have the option to say nothing, end the conversation, and walk away.

## Healing Tool 9:
## Tips to Help You Set and Achieve Goals

*Tip 1: Develop Your Personal Action and Accountability Plan*

This plan is your road map to achieving goals, getting where you want to go, and getting back on course when you get lost. Remember that your character, people skills, personal limitations, emotional makeup, and motivation level will impact achievement of goals. Mentors and coaches can help you generate your action plan, monitor your progress, hold you accountable, and develop alternate course of actions when you hit roadblocks. The value of a coach is obvious to anyone who has watched his or her home team come back to win a title after a dismal losing streak. To develop your road map, take the following steps:

1. Write your goals down and set realistic target dates for completing them, taking into account your other commitments in life. Set goals to be the best you can be in all aspects of your life, including finances, family, spirituality, physical health, relationships, careers, social life, and community. Be sure to include short-term goals (three to six months) as well as long-term goals so you will quickly have a feeling of success. Short-term goals

might include taking a class, researching a new business, or finding an exercise buddy or coach who will keep you motivated and accountable.
2. Add a target date for completing each goal.
3. Evaluate how close you are right now to achieving your short- and long-term goals. Have you achieved 10 percent of your goal or possibly even 90 percent? Identify what you need to do to fill the gap to get you to 100 percent. Remember how success will feel or sound to you when you reach 100 percent. How will you or your loved ones benefit from achieving your goals?
4. Under or next to each goal, make a chronological list of the actions you need to take to achieve the goal. Include a target date next to each action.
5. Monitor your progress. Record and date the status next to each action. Evaluate what actions you started, which you completed, and what is stopping you from completing the others. Add sub-actions where needed to get you back on track.
6. Try not to change any due dates unless absolutely necessary. Continually changing dates can give you a false sense of security that you are on target, effective, and accountable when in fact you are not.
7. Periodically assess all aspects of your life and set new goals as needed.

*Tip 2: Make Sure Your Goals Work for You*

Change is never comfortable. In life, whatever we want to achieve has to have clear benefits. Otherwise, the challenges we face will seem impossible to overcome and not worth the effort. What are the short- and long-term benefits of achieving your goals? Identifying these benefits is essential to staying committed to achieving your goals. Success must feel good; otherwise, you will not be motivated to change.

The benefits will be different for each of us because we process information and experiences differently. Success will feel, sound, smell, and look differently to everyone. How will success look to you? How will you know you are getting closer to achieving your short-term and long-term goals?

*Tip 3: Identify Your Challenges*

You are sure to face challenges and obstacles along the way that can stop you dead in your tracks. Have you identified these? What are they, and how will you deal with them or at least minimize their impact? What will you have to give up or change to achieve your goals? Are you, for example, good at delaying gratification? Do you have the self-discipline needed to succeed? If not, how will you stay on track? Perhaps you have a good friend or can hire a life coach to keep you honest. There may be people who should not know about your goals. Do you have people like this in your life?

*Tip 4: Set Realistic Goals*

Goals must be attainable to be achievable. For example, I will never become a high jumper because I do not have the build, desire, or genetics to be one. We must be aware of our personal limitations when we are setting our goals so as to avoid setting ourselves up for failure.

On the other hand, we must overcome invisible psychological barriers that prevent us from setting and attaining goals. Mentors and coaches can help you identify and distinguish the differences between your limits and your limitations that both can prevent you from achieving happiness in your life.

*Tip 5: Resist the Urge to Consider Accountability to Your Healing Goals as Shame*

Learn to replace your triggered shame with a healthier dose of guilt, which empowers you to take responsibility and course-correct and seek help to achieve your milestones, intermediate targets and final goals. As Michael A. Wright, PhD, advises in "Accountability Is Not Shame, but Guilt Can Be Motivating":

> When you feel you have fallen short, determine whether you are responding to guilt or shame. If you are responding to guilt you will ask, "What choices did I make that were not in line with my goals? What choices can I make now to move sustainably toward my goals?" If you are responding to shame and engaging in conflict you will exclaim, "There are many reasons why I am not achieving my goals! Few people understand my struggle."

# Appendix 2

# Inspirational Healing Messages

Trauma creates change you *don't* choose. Healing is about creating change you *do* choose.—Michele Rosenthal

Abuse is never your fault. It is not your shame to carry.—Anne-Marie Wiesman

Often a good heart doesn't see a bad heart coming. Forgive yourself for the harm someone's done you.—Karen Salmansohn

You cannot heal at the same level of thinking that creates your pain.—Evelyn Ryan

Whatever is happening in your life, don't preoccupy yourself with the question "why"? But rather ponder more on to where these events will be bringing you. Know that you are being led to somewhere beautiful beyond your present harsh reality. Once you get to the where, then you'll know the why.—Karen Salmansohn

Growth is a forceful evolution. It isn't a gentle process. I didn't find giving birth completely gentle and peaceful. Rather it was an essential force for my baby and me. It harnessed the sheer vitality life insists on to flourish.—Alfie Stone

Using someone else's ruler to measure your self-worth will always leave you short.—Charles F. Glassman

When we know better and know we are worthy of the knowledge, we do better.—Evelyn Ryan

> The Optimist's Creed
> Christian D. Larson

Promise yourself …
To be so strong that nothing can disturb your peace of mind.
To talk health, happiness, and prosperity to every person you meet.

To make all your friends feel that there is something worthwhile in them.
To look at the sunny side of everything and make your optimism come true.
To think only of the best, to work only for the best, and to expect only the best.
To be just as enthusiastic about the success of others as you are about your own.
To forget the mistakes of the past and press on to the greater achievements of the future.
To wear a cheerful expression at all times and give a smile to every living creature you meet.
To give so much time to improving yourself that you have no time to criticize others.
To be too large for worry, too noble for anger, too strong for fear, and too happy to permit the presence of trouble.
To think well of yourself and to proclaim this fact to the world, not in loud word, but in great deeds.
To live in the faith that the whole world is on your side, so long as you are true to the best that is in you.

## The Gentleman
### Sheri Spain

I've met the most amazing gentleman, the man of my deepest dreams and desires.
Kindness, understanding, attentive. Handsome, giving, intelligent.
A true gentleman who walks me safely to my car.
I'm fragile, I say. I've had loss.
I'll never hurt you, he assures.
Love overwhelms quickly, I share my awe with one and all.
He's a gentleman, truly. My hero. My partner. My man. My soul mate. My king.

I am the queen of his world, he says. I'm twitterpated. Quotes from Bambi?! Yes! Oh, my.
Marry me. Yes.
The nightmare begins softly, the very next week.
An ugly word or two. Uncharacteristic inconsideration. Excuses, apologies, gifts. Ignoring, complaining, forgetting. Intimacy withheld.
I'm sorry, I'm sorry, I love you. Don't leave me.
What is wrong with me? His cries work their deceit.
It's okay, I murmur. We are committed, we'll work this out.
I should have listened to myself, my intuition, nagging concerns.
Tantrums, crazy-making, nonsensical demands commence.
My needs are dismissed, his concerns the only priority.
I'm sorry, I'm sorry, I love you. Don't leave me.
What is wrong with me?
We mustn't tell, no one will like me, he fears. He cries and moans.
Shares his agonies of life, such sadness and pain and tragedy.
A victim, many times over, at the hands of women. Psycho-bitches all.
I see and feel. Deeply. A knowing. A gift and a curse.
I give in. I trust again. Benefit of the doubt. Again. Stupid.
I'll get help, he says. I'll tell the truth.
Promises, promises, promises. Promises never ever kept, never ever meant. Just carrots dangling.
His secret became my secret. My burden to bear
While his adoring fans gather 'round. Rock star fantasy lives.
He quits his meds, dismisses his doctors. (He lied to them, too.)
Escalating crisis, erratic behavior. Danger dances. A roller coaster, ever-jumping tracks. Chaos reigns. He rules.
Alone, so alone. Suffocating in shallow and fallacy.
I call his adult daughter to encourage and support her dad. She's sorry. She's not equipped to handle these behaviors he's been plagued with all his life.
Shock, just shock. Manipulated. I'm not the first, second, or third.

Another discard, another souvenir. A serial abuser of women. A master manipulator.

Fear is the cacophony. No more mask at home. His Bundy is released. Charm and torture. He controls my food, my activities, when I can sleep.

Me. I'm dying as the servant of his twisted facade. Sucking me dry.

A vampire.

Forceful isolation. Degradation. Humiliation. Fear becomes terror. His fists come out. My tears and pain belittled.

An accident, I didn't mean to, I don't remember. It's your fault. I've cowered in corners, his spittle in my face, finger poking my bones.

I've hidden weapons from him and slept in my car. Concealed the bruises. Keeping the secret. Codependent.

I try and try and try and try and try and try and try and try. I read and research and read some more while he saunters. And smirks. Does nothing. While I work. And work. And work.

Maybe this will work, maybe that will change. Maybe, maybe. Accept the reality; let go of the dream. Turn to the cliff. Jump.

I tell him I'm done. He steals my resume, my writing. Spends the last of my money. Hoards his. Bribes for his minions.

Trapped. Scared. Don't make him mad. Misery.

Months and months.

John Q matters significantly, I am nothing. Never was. Just a pawn.

His fury grows with non-reaction, upping the ante until I fight back.

He smiles with his victory hand; his game complete. Demonized.

It's fun making you lose your mind, my tormentor taunts.

Go ahead and tell, no one will believe you. You're the crazy one, he says. Not me. I'm a shaman and an alchemist. And a man of God.

My tribe says so. They say there's nothing wrong with me. Sneer.

I understand. I get it. More lessons to be revealed.
For they all love the most amazing gentleman they've ever met. Who never was.

> If you are depressed, you are living in the past. If you are anxious, you are living in the future. If you are at peace, you are living in the present.—Lao Tzu
>
> Courage for survivors of abuse is replacing the pain and fear with faith in ourselves, an understanding that we are worth the self-sacrifice for truth, and trust that we deserve the outcomes of our efforts.—Evelyn Ryan
>
> We begin to heal when the sunshine and fog break through the fog, bringing with them the hope of freeing our souls like the sky to show their true colors again.—Evelyn Ryan
>
> Healing is a rough journey. It is like finding your way through the desert without a map or landmarks. But like water and shade, our courage and trust in ourselves and our will to live sustain us. And in that journey, we discover who we really are, what we are capable of, and what our purpose is. And we not only survive … we thrive.—Evelyn Ryan
>
> There is a big difference between living from a core of truth and personal self-worth and living from a core of lies where you need assurance that what you believe is the truth and what you do is worthy.—Evelyn Ryan
>
> Coming into truth after living in lies is like finally figuring out a magic trick. You thought it was real but now you know it was all an illusion.—Evelyn Ryan
>
> "No" is a complete sentence. It does not need justification or explanation.—Unknown
>
> Believing a lie does not make it truth, and not believing the truth does not make it a lie.—Evelyn Ryan
>
> Fools take a knife and stab people in the back. The wise take the knife, cut the cord, and free themselves from the fools.—Karen Salmansohn

You don't have to have it all figured out to move forward.—Unknown

There is nothing noble about being superior to another person. True nobility is being superior to the person you once were.—Unknown

Make this your personal motto: "I am an unstoppable warrior who is strong and fearless. I live with courage and compassion in my heart. I wear my confidence like a shield to deflect all negativity. I am powerful and proud of who I am and what I do. I wake up each day positive and ready to take on the day ahead because I am on a mission to achieve my goals and nothing and no one can stop me."

The silence feeds the shame. Tell your story. You will inspire others.—Anne-Marie Wiesman

There is no coming into consciousness without pain. People will do nothing, no matter how absurd, in order to avoid facing their own soul. One does not become enlightened by imagining figures of light, but by making the darkness conscious.—Carl G. Jung

This is what enlightenment and consciousness raising are all about. Owning our power to be a co-creator of our lives by changing our relationship with ourselves. We can change the way we think. We can change the way we respond to our own emotions. We need to detach from our wounded self in order to allow our Spiritual Self to guide us. We are Unconditionally Loved. The Spirit does not speak to us from judgment and shame.—Robert Burney

Your brain's sole job is to find you proof of what you tell it. The more you tell it you will find a way the more it will look for ways to make that be the truth. When you start seeing the evidence of this truth (in even the tiniest moments) you will start building up a core connection to both your Core Self and self-belief that leads you ever closer to healing and The New You.—Michele Rosenthal

My power is made perfect in weakness … we are filled with contempt, our soul full of scorn of the arrogant and disdain of the proud … That from our weakness we arise like a phoenix and remain faithful and hopeful in the Word.—2 Corinthians 12:7-10

# Bibliography

Bower, Sharon Anthony, and Gordon H. Bower. *Asserting Yourself—Updated Edition: A Practical Guide for Positive Change.* 2nd ed. Boston, MA: Da Capo Press, 2004.

Carnes, Patrick. *The Betrayal Bond: Breaking Free of Exploitive Relationships.* Deerfield Beach, FL: Health Communications. 1997.

Evans, Melanie Tonia. "The Difference Between the Inner Child and the Ego." *Narcissism and Relationships Blog.* April 3, 2014. http://blog.melanietoniaevans.com/the-difference-between-the-inner-child-and-the-ego/.

Frances, Allen. "When Good Grief Goes Bad" (interview with Dr. Holly Prigerson). *The Blog.* Huffington Post. February 28, 2012. http://www.huffingtonpost.com/allen-frances/grief-depression_b_1301050.html.

Gannon, J. Patrick, et. al. *ASCA Survivor to Thriver Manual.* 4th ed. San Francisco, CA: The Norma J. Morris Center, 2007. http://www.ascasupport.org/_html_manuals/survivortothriver/indexSurvivorManual.html.

Hall, Karyn. "Understanding Shame." *PsychCentral.* June 22, 2012. http://blogs.psychcentral.com/emotionally-sensitive/2012/06/understanding-shame/.

Hein, Steven. "Emotional Validation." *EQI.org.* http://eqi.org/valid.htm.

Lancer, Darlene. *Conquering Shame and Codependency: 8 Steps to Freeing the True You.* Center City, MN: Hazleton, 2014.

McGregor, Jane, and Tim McGregor. "Empathic People Are Natural Targets for Sociopaths—Protect Yourself." *Addiction Today*. October 10, 2013. http://www.sott.net/article/268449-Empathic-people-are-natural-targets-for-sociopaths-protect-yourself.

Saeed, Kim. "Narcissists and Empaths: The Ego Dynamic." *Letmereach.com*. April 16, 2014. http://letmereach.com/2014/04/16/narcissists-and-empaths-the-ego-dynamic/.

Sherwood, Glynis. "Emotional Sobriety: The Golden Key to Addiction Recovery." *Glynissherwood.com*. March 18, 2013. http://www.glynissherwood.com/blog/emotional-sobriety-the-golden-key-to-addiction-recovery.

———. "Stop the Struggle: Five Steps to Breaking Free from Chronic Emotional Pain." *Glynissherwood.com*. 2012. http://www.glynissherwood.com/resources/Free%20Report%20-%20Stop%20the%20Struggle%20-%20Glynis%20Sherwood%20-%20May%202012.pdf.

Simon, George K., Jr. *Character Disturbance: The Phenomenon of Our Age*. Little Rock: Parkhurst Brothers, Inc. 2011.

Sirota, Marcia. "Post Traumatic Stress in Adult Survivors of Child Abuse." *Post-Traumatic Stress Disorder—Adult Survivors of Child Abuse* (blog). August 25, 2006. http://adultsurvivors.blogspot.com/2006/08/post-traumatic-stress-in-adult.html.

van der Kolk, Bessel. *The Body Keeps the Score: Brain, Mind, and Body in the Healing of Trauma*. New York: Penguin Group, 2014.

Walker, Pete. "Shrinking the Inner Critic in Complex PTSD." PeteWalker.com. May 1, 2015. http://www.pete-walker.com.

Wax, Dustin. "The Science of Setting Goals." *Lifehack.* February 2015. http://www.lifehack.org/articles/productivity/the-science-of-setting-goals.html.

Wright, Michael A. "Accountability Is Not Shame, but Guilt Can Be Motivating." *Coach Method.* July 7, 2013. http://mawmedia.com/COACHMethod/2013/07/05/accountability-is-not-shame-but-guilt-can-be-motivating/.

Made in the USA
Middletown, DE
22 February 2017